WIDOWER

WIDOWER

Kenneth Richardson

First trade paperback edition published 2025.

Printed in the United States of America and other countries.

larquepress.com

ISBN: 978-1-7372299-5-7

10 9 8 7 6 5 4 3 2 1

LAR
1952–2023

Months Seventeen to Twenty-Four

My Afterlife

Appendices

Introduction

L was my best friend for over 50 years and my wife for over 48. Her death in 2023 devastated me. I sought numerous sources for help and support as I grappled with my grief and tried to make sense of the loss. This book is the story of my journey.

Shortly after her death, I met with a good friend of hers, who had lost his wife less than two years earlier. Craig and I had met a few times over the years due to his collaboration with L when she was a freelance designer; and as her coworker prior to that. He was gracious enough to meet with me to discuss our losses. Our talk was invaluable to me for his understanding of this territory; and comforting because he also felt the loss of his friend and colleague. There is nothing like talking to someone who has dealt with a devastating loss themselves, and in particular, the same loss.

When our son Colin died, it felt emotionally like being run over by a truck. As L and I slowly began to learn how to live with his loss, I turned to writing. I thought that I would write a book as therapy for myself, and to honor Colin's memory. I wrote a few thousand words over a series of weeks, but life's demands intervened and I never finished.

Then, 35 years later, I was again overwhelmed by loss. Over the following two years I have turned to writing to help deal with my grief and try to grasp what a life alone means. I wrote often in diary form directed to L, recording my feelings and recounting daily tasks as if she was still here to read the words.

After a career as a copywriter and project manager, I was now better equipped to write a book than I was in 1988. But I'm also just a typical, once happily married husband and father. I'm special to my family and friends, but quite ordinary in the larger sense. I think that is part of why this book may be useful. I wrote it to help myself deal with my afterlife, to honor the memory of my wife, and to be of some help and comfort to those who find themselves suddenly grieving the loss of their spouse.

This is an epistolary book. Some of its content

is specially included for the bereaved's adjustments to living alone, but it is also a love letter to my wife about my journey in grief. The reflections are roughly linear, but at times shift back-and-forth at points along my path. That feels right, because that's the herky-jerky rhythm of grief itself.

Although there are similarities for each loss, every death and every grief is unique. So are their timelines. People in grief experience similar feelings and emotions and nod theirs heads in agreement when they recognize one person's experience with an analogous one of their own. Some elements are of major importance to one person's grief, while being relatively minor for someone else. For example, guilt may haunt the husband whose wife committed suicide, while guilt may not loom large in a death caused by a fatal disease. The challenges of grief occur in waves, and their arrival is unpredictable.

This memoir documents my first two years alone. My journey is not a roadmap for yours. My experience is offered in the hope that parts will resonate for you and provide some solace, understanding, and hope as you move through the valley and find your way forward alone.

Some may wonder why there is a detailed section in the middle on my cataract surgery. First, there are a lot of seniors who will have to face this experience themselves, so perhaps my report will be useful. Second, it was the first major health event I faced without my wife, another reality of the widower.

For orientation's sake, Harry is our son, Colin too, Whitney is our daughter, and Sean is our son-in-law. Louise is my sister, and Kent is my brother-in-law. L had no siblings.

Over our many years together L and I traded quips and "catch phrases" gleaned from popular culture, invented, or adopted unconsciously from whereabouts unknown. These were often transient, and what was timely at one point, eventually fell out of use. But a handful endured. They feel like treasures now that she's no longer here to add to our personal culture.

Inspired by the neighbors to the north of our home state, we adopted "uff da" into our vernacular after seeing the movie *Fargo*. I probably used the expression more often, but when I did, L would nearly always concur with "Uff da, indeed."

When we entered the pandemic, she'd often refer to our old normal world as the "before times." I always liked that reference, but I'm afraid it now encompasses our past lives together.

L was a fan of several of the "housewives" shows, where she picked up the idiom "nicey nice," usually expressed with sarcasm. She also introduced me to "This is why we can't have nice things," an appropriate comment after a spill, or when our puppy left a "present" on the carpet.

She loved animals and pets, and we had more than less during our years together raising our kids. In her final years she'd praise Whitney and Sean's dog, and later our bulldog, with the endearment "champion" as in "What a little champion." Or if I said, "Good dog." She'd respond with, "A little champion, really."

When something needed further investigation, she'd often preface the notion with, "Let's just take a little looksee." And when identifying a flavor, instead of commenting it has "a hint of orange," she'd say it has, "a whisper of orange."

We overheard the mother of a car full of kids about to begin their holiday visit at their grandparent's house remark, "All right, smiles everyone!" We grabbed onto that line in a heartbeat.

When we'd watched a particularly intense drama before bed, we'd follow it with a short, light "palate cleanser" to reset, like an episode of *The Office*.

L and Whitney both painted square wooden blocks for our library's annual fund raiser. In 2023, L included a few words along with images of a raven or a sheep. "Be kind" was the epitome of the way she lived her life. "Ewe be ewe" was a playful twist that made a popular affirmation her own.

L's Grandmother was fond of noting, "I'm not fussy, but I know what I like." L adopted the phrase as her own, and it served her well for decades.

For me, these phrases are gems. I'll treasure them for the rest of my days, and when recalled—along with so many other reminders—I will think of my love and honor her memory by keeping them alive.

Months One to Eight
Decent Into Death

My Dearest Love: When I knew that you would die soon, I held onto the feeling that it could somehow be denied. Like your death itself, it was a strange limbo, an unreality, a mentality that this can't be happening. How could you be here one moment and gone the next? How could I remain, if you could not? As I watched you slip away, I was helpless.

Going back a year or two, I knew you were suffering with chronic pain. A bad hip that slowly got worse over the years. Your distrust of doctors led you to massage, acupuncture, physical therapy, and yoga. You did your exercises every day, and took aspirin often, if not daily. Eventually, the yoga became too painful and was abandoned. You were stoic and seldom complained. I asked you how you felt most days. You acknowledged your difficulties but never dwelt on them aloud or expressed self-pity. You nearly always focused on the positive. Your leadership was nearly always by example. Ernest Hemingway could've meant you when he wrote, "You are so brave and quiet I forget you are suffering."

When there were no alternatives left, you began the search for a doctor. You found a general practitioner who referred you to a hip surgeon. An appointment was scheduled, at last. A few days later, your urine was much darker than normal. You called, and your GP directed you to the emergency room.

Tests revealed excess bile. Scans revealed a mass on your gall bladder. They moved you from waiting rooms to a bed in a shared room in the hospital. A procedure to insert a plastic tube into your bile duct was done to increase the flow. You were sedated, but this was a minimally invasive procedure with a quick recovery. Your urine returned to normal immediately.

I don't remember the exact order of events, but they wanted to transfer you from Vancouver to Providence Hospital in Portland, where specialists had more expertise directly related to the problem.

Further tests revealed cancer of the gall bladder. Ugh. To release you from PeaceHealth and have you reenter the queue at Providence from home would result in a lower priority status, so they held you at PeaceHealth so your path into Providence would be high priority. We were hopeful and anxious to move to Providence as quickly as possible.

Your stay at PeaceHealth for the better part of a week was comfortable, but monotonous. You shared a room. Your roommate was in pain, and her moans made the first few days and nights challenging. She'd been on dialysis for several years, and it never worked well for her. Her daughter was her advocate and had arranged for someone to come and talk to her about end-of-life care.

Only a few feet and a curtain separated us, so we heard the discussion. The doctor/advisor confirmed that dialysis is not effective for everyone. Some tolerate it well, others do not. This poor woman was tired of fighting and opted for hospice, where, without dialysis she would die quickly. The priority would be to keep her comfortable.

I spent the days with you but went home before dinner to tend to the home front. I wasn't there when they moved your roommate out. The next day she was gone, and the bed was empty. There was less tension in the air. We chatted and even watched a little TV together, still waiting to hear when your transfer would come.

It was the time of year for senior flu shots and Covid boosters. I went one day and got both. We deferred yours for better days.

Things progressed after you moved to Providence. You were lucky to settle into one of the best rooms in the hospital. It was a huge, private room with a bed, recliner, two side chairs, and a table. It was on the top floor with a commanding view. Directly below was the interstate highway, but beyond you could see houses and lots of trees. The sunshine beaming in gave us hope. The food was a bit better here as well, and you chose fresh vegetables, berries, and yogurt.

Then the worst news came. The cancer had spread. After several more scans and tests it was deemed inoperable. It had spread too far and would have to be treated with chemotherapy and radiation.

They sent you home, which was your only real relief at this point. In the following week you had a procedure to have a portal installed on your chest. The portal would provide quick access to your circulatory system in preparation for chemo. They also used it for the anesthetic when you had a biopsy to determine the exact type of cancer that was spreading through your body. Even though there was a fairly quick succession of appointments, the process of getting to a complete diagnosis and then to the treatment plan seemed to drag on when all we wanted was to begin the treatment, to fight back, immediately.

I helped you relocate from our bedroom to the family room with the TV, from the couch to the armchair and back again, as you changed your position or location often to relieve your discomfort. I kept your meds coming as needed and brought food and liquids. We watched TV when you felt well enough to focus. The last movie we saw together was *Uncle Buck*, one of our favorites. I made a list of others.

I remember you shaking your head at one point and saying, "I am so not a cancer person." I think that was because there was remarkably no history of cancer in your family, that I can recall. No wonder it seemed so alien. Like you, I was shocked, disoriented, and helpless.

The next complication was vomiting and nausea. A call to your primary doctor sent us back to the emergency room at PeaceHealth. They inserted a tube into your nose that ran down into your stomach so they could drain it. It was somewhat uncomfortable for you, but you were partially sedated and it relieved the symptoms you'd developed. You were your usual brave, good-natured self—a terrific patient.

Again, they determined to move you to Providence, so we waited around for the ambulance to take you. They had decided to leave the tube in during the transfer. By that time, it had relieved the issue it was supposed to, so I felt like they should remove it. However, I didn't push the point.

As the EMTs moved you from your hospital bed to a stretcher, the tube was inadvertently pulled out, and thankfully not reinserted. I was glad you didn't have to suffer the discomfort of that thing any longer. By now it was late and would likely be 2:00 AM before your arrival at Providence, let alone getting situated in a room. We agreed I would go home and come over in the morning. You assured me you'd be okay. You texted your room number once you had it.

Your new room was in a closed-off area for cancer patients. You had trouble sleeping for some time at this point and laying in bed was very uncomfortable. The nurse located a large reclining chair and arranged for it to be brought to your room. We both breathed a sigh of relief when it arrived, and you got situated. A small thing, but one of the few within our control. Of course, you were getting meds too, so your discomfort was lessened considerably.

They ran more tests and scans, and the lead doctor gave us the news in the morning. The cancer had grown rapidly and aggressively. Even he was surprised how quickly it had spread into all of the surrounding organs, creating obstructions to your bladder (again) and bowels. He prefaced his list of your options by admitting none were good. You could have a colostomy bag, he could connect your stomach directly to your large intestine, or you could elect hospice care. The medical options sounded like a real-life Frankenstein's monster. More pain and discomfort, for what? The cancer was now untreatable. An operation might extend your life by a few weeks, but they'd be miserable weeks. You opted for hospice care at home, and I agreed. It was the only real choice.

There are many things about hospice that are good, but perhaps the most important thing is that the doctors and nurses don't have to consider drug addiction, they can medicate you freely and focus on comfort over all else. I don't remember why they kept you at Providence one more night, but when I came back in the morning, you'd been moved out of the cancer ward into another room. We waited there while your paperwork was wrapped up, and you could be released. We were glad you were coming home, but we knew it would be final. This hospital room would be the last one you would ever see.

A nurse wheeled you out and settled you on a bench outside at the curb while I took your belongings out and brought the car around.

At home we set up a makeshift recliner using our big green armchair, with oversized pillows to support your back at a comfortable angle and your legs slightly elevated off the floor. A hospice nurse came in a few hours and outlined their services and gave us their 24-hour call number. Meds and equipment were arranged and began arriving that day and the next. Their goal was your comfort, which was mine as well. I was determined to do as much as possible to limit your pain.

Initially, it seemed like we'd see a nurse every other day or perhaps less often, but as the seriousness of your condition became apparent, they sent a nurse every day and if I'm remembering correctly maybe even twice on some days.

Whitney found a spiral-bound planner that we

used to record and schedule all your meds and milestones. In addition to multiple pain relievers, there were laxatives, anti-nausea meds, and tranquilizers. I was surprised that ordinary Tylenol was part of the pain meds, but apparently it works very well in conjunction with the more powerful ones. Over the course of your short remaining time your pain meds included oxycodone, morphine, and methadone.

The hospice provided equipment like a hospital bed, supplies like wipes and vomit tubes, and all the meds delivered directly to our door. The meds in particular came within hours after they were ordered, for which I will always be grateful.

Whitney and Sean were in the process of having their house completely remodeled, so they had moved in with us during this period. I was so thankful to have them here during your final days, and afterward when I was on my own. Sean still had to work, telecommuting from a make-shift office upstairs. Harry and Whitney and I were your nurses, guided by the hospice team. Both kids were on extended leaves from their work, so we were here around the clock for you. Harry was working swing shift at the time, so he was used to being up all night. I jokingly referred to him as your night nurse, but I'm grateful one of us was always available to you at any hour.

You weren't sleeping well in spite of all the meds, catching only an hour or two of sleep throughout the days and nights. Your nausea and vomiting continued, perhaps better due to the meds, but never completely gone.

I'd planned to invite our best friends over to visit you over a series of days, but I only had time to make arrangements for one couple. I'm so grateful you got to see them one last time before you died. I'm sorry we never made it to the others, or to a video call with your lifelong friend Lucia.

On your second day home we made your last trip outside the house, to remove the portal. During these first few days your diet consisted of toast, banana, crackers, berries, and yogurt. These were more like snacks than meals. You had water at your side around the clock. You took the laxative senna every day, but it wasn't working. You weren't eating very much, but the head nurse was concerned.

We'd moved you from the TV room into the yoga room. (The house's formal dining room that we used for yoga.) Whitney hurriedly made curtains, and Sean helped her hang them, so you had some privacy against the previously bare windows.

By the eighth day your doses had been increased, and we switched anything that had been in pill form to liquid, because swallowing was difficult. You still struggled with vomiting in spite of the prochlorperazine and the scopolamine patch. I think this was the day a social worker came along with the nurse. She sat down with Harry, Whitney, and I in the TV room and presented options for local funeral homes, hospice counseling services, and offered a visit from their chaplain.

No one wanted to take pictures of you in your weakened state, but the social worker suggested we take hold your hand and take a picture of that. Whitney and I liked the idea, and we took our final pictures of you.

I know Whitney spent some time with you and told you how much you meant to her. I tried to do the same multiple times but was unable to speak each time I tried. I hope you saw the depth of my love for you in my misty eyes and choked voice. Watching your decline was like watching Colin's so, so long ago. Feeling utter helplessness. A living nightmare, without hope.

Despite the tube, your bile duct was still compromised. The amount you were able to pee didn't offset all of the liquids you were drinking, so your legs began to swell. As the nurse told us, the water had to go somewhere. In another day, your legs began to "sweat." It was better if they were elevated, but that was too uncomfortable for you, so most often your legs were down which made the swelling worse. We put calf-length compression socks on your legs to help counteract the swelling. The cloth became soaked with water in a matter of minutes. My heart ached to see yet another symptom of your suffering.

On your last Friday, you took a shower to freshen up. The hospice had provided a wheelchair, and I imagine that was how Harry and I got you up and down the stairs, but honestly, I don't remember. I know the shower took an effort, but you got through it and felt better to be fresh.

Whitney had hoped to arrange for a hairdresser to come and do your hair, but it become obvious that it wasn't going to happen. Instead, she braided your hair so it could be down, but out of your way.

By Saturday you were talking less and seemed less aware. The increased dosage of pain meds and tranqs were fogging your brain. I hated this was happening so quickly but remained adamant that pain relief was the greatest priority.

For several days, the head nurse was determined to move you from the armchair to the hospital bed. I didn't understand her insistence but eventually capitulated. She arranged several layers of sheets so we could move you by clutching the sheets instead of trying to pick you up. Sean and I did the heavy tugging while she layered pillows around you for support, so you could sit upright. In hindsight, I think the nurse felt it would be a better place to die; in a temporary bed that would be returned to the hospital rather than a family chair that might permanently be associated with your death from then on.

You stopped eating and drank only 6 ounces of water on your last full day. I learned later this is normal as the body prepares itself for death. We administered the liquid meds with eye droppers, dripping them into your mouth between gums and cheek. They're absorbed directly and don't need to be swallowed, which you no longer could do. And you were no longer talking, just breathing in raspy breathes through your open mouth. Also normal at this stage. The hospice had provided little sponges on sticks that we used to swab inside your mouth to keep it at least somewhat moist. We attended you often, but death was near.

I hadn't slept very well for several nights. I went

to bed at about 8 o'clock and set my alarm for midnight, a few minutes before another round of oxycodone and lorazepam. When I came downstairs, Harry was upset. You'd slumped forward and he was struggling to keep you sitting upright. I took over and removed one of the pillows behind you, guiding you back until you seemed comfortable and relaxed. Your labored breathing sent a pang of sorrow through my heart. I used a pulse oximeter to check your vitals. Your heart rate was very rapid, and your oxygen level had dropped into the 70s. I knew this couldn't go on for much longer, but there was nothing that could be done.

We administered your meds with eye droppers and hovered around you. I probably moistened your mouth with a stick sponge again, but I don't remember. At 1:15 am you stopped breathing. The oximeter verified that you'd died. I told Harry you'd gone and asked him to go upstairs and wake Whitney and Sean. I called the hospice and told them what had happened. They said they'd send a nurse, who arrived before too long.

You could have died at any time the previous day or while I was sleeping, but I believe you waited for me to return to your side before you let go. We were an almost unbreakable pair for so long,

I don't think you would have left without me beside you. It may sound like a small thing in the
greater scheme, but I'll always be grateful you held
on for me.

When the nurse arrived, she went to work immediately, cleaning and arranging your body on
the hospital bed. She asked which funeral home
we'd selected and called them before she left.

We returned to your side, one by one to say our
final goodbyes. Despite all that had preceded, I was
dazed by the stark reality of your death. I pulled a
chair over to your side and held your lifeless hand.
You were the best friend I ever had. It was such a
privilege to have shared so much of your life. You
were my compass, my confidant, my great love,
and mother of our children.

I don't know where your spirit went. Were you
still here in the room with me? Were you looking
down on me as I wept, or had you floated away
when you left this world behind to explore the
wonders promised in the afterlife. I felt no certain-
ty, only hope that you still could exist in some better place.

You were a role model throughout your ordeal.
If you ever thought of yourself, you never voiced
a complaint, spat out an order, or shouted at any-

one to "just leave me alone!" Your concerns were always for others, me in particular. What would happen to me once you weren't here to take care of me? I know I can take care of any day-to-day stuff, but how will I find the will to go on without you? Every time I hear or see something to share, who will I tell? Who will care what I think, like you did? I'm afraid the answer is no one.

Each of us, individually said our goodbyes, and we sat in the adjacent room or paced as we waited. The funeral attendant arrived shortly and wheeled in a gurney. He was a big man so I knew he wouldn't need my help with your body. He transferred you from the hospital bed into a body bag and onto the gurney. Only your face was visible. He gave us a few more minutes for a final goodbye, then rolled you out of the front door and into the hearse.

After a short while, we split up and returned to our bedrooms. If I know myself, I probably poured a couple of shots of gin into a glass and sat up in our bed, drinking, trying to grasp this new reality. I don't remember.

In our final heart-to-heart you reflected that you'd had a good life. You were grateful for our marriage and our children, our son-in-law, and friends. I'm grateful for your courage and calm as you faced your mortality. As so often in your life, you shared your best self with the world.

Whitney told me that in her last conversation with you, you said your biggest worry about us was how I would get along without you. Even now, writing these words, I have tears in my eyes. I hope you know how much you meant to me, now, and during all our years together. I love you, I love you, I love you, my sweet, sweet angel.

Survivor's Guilt

My Love: Your death was both terribly real and somehow unreal. A living nightmare one moment and a foggy cloud the next. How could this be happening? I was devastated by sorrow and an unexpected feeling of guilt. How was it possible I was still here, and you weren't? How could I deserve to live after you were gone?

I've never experienced survivor's guilt before, but now it seems ever present. A few nights after you died, Whitney, Sean, and I sat in front of the TV and started to watch season one of *Dark Winds*. You and I had seen this together in 2022. I felt oddly guilty. Why do I get to relive this stellar show? How is it that I get to share this time with our family and you do not?

A few days later I went to our credit union and had your name taken off our accounts and CU credit card. The clerk was condolent and efficient. Logically, it was the right thing to do, but it felt like betrayal. It felt as if I was party to an effort to erase your existence.

Working through the tasks to straighten up our affairs was draining. I could only do a little at a time. I had to stop and direct my attention elsewhere, or I'd lose patience, or plunge deeper into the gloom that already hung over everything.

Harry, Whitney, and I had agreed on cremation, as you had directed. I decided against any kind of ceremony. Harry and Whitney agreed. I felt guilt over this too. None of your friends were allowed the kind of closure that might occur at a wake. I couldn't face organizing one, and I was convinced it would have been torture for me, so I denied others the chance to gather to mourn your passing.

Your ashes are now in a box in your closet. Harry, Whitney, Sean and I will disperse your cremains at sea next summer. It will be a private ceremony. I feel okay about that. I'll notify friends when it's happening. It will give them a specific time to remember and reflect on what you meant to them. Maybe you'll feel their collective energy, wherever you are.

I read online there's some shocking statistic about the percentage of people who die within three weeks of their spouse. Yesterday, it was three weeks since you died, so at least I've made it this far. A good friend's wife died suddenly a few years ago. He was devastated. He lived for a year or a year and half after she died. He had a stroke and died a few days later. I can't help wondering if that will be me a year and a half from now.

Should I have been more forceful with you a year ago about your hip?

Should I have pushed you to see a doctor long before cancer? I could have, but I knew your faith in medicine, so I left you to decide for yourself. After all, what could I say that was more motivating than your pain? Even knowing that, I can't help wondering if your chronic discomfort wore you down, gnawing an opening for cancer to exploit somewhere else in your body. Self-blame is so inviting. A point of focus to cover up the reality of utter helplessness. To take it on as my fault. To imagine a way in which none of this never happened.

As tempting as it is to withdraw inside supposition, I can't live in what might have been. Did your suffering force you to confront your mortality and turn your mind toward fatalism, preparing you to deal with cancer when it appeared? I'll never know. Fate is no one's fault. Fate is random and unpredictable, and it's scary to think our lives are only skating along the rim of the abyss.

These feelings of survivor's guilt have come and gone to varying degrees of intensity during the weeks since your death. But they return—if less often—even months later.

Cards and emails from friends have been comforting. Marc and Jessica sent a beautiful bouquet. Thankfully, our peeps are a sensitive lot, so there weren't any oddball comments or upsets. It's easy to have expectations, but therapists advise that expectations can quickly turn into resentment when they aren't met. Better not to expect anything. That's good advice in general, and something you've told me more than once.

We can be our own worst enemies and set too many expectations for ourselves in grief. Why can't I let go? I should be stronger. I should move on at a certain point. But then, what if I haven't? I try to release my expectations and calm my mind.

The cousin of guilt is shame. Shame thrives in

secrecy. Finding a moment of joy in the shadow of grief can stir feelings of shame. In these early days, shame follows every smile or laugh, smothering it in guilt. I take a breath and remind myself to let go and forgive myself as I would anyone else on this path. It's so challenging to accept this new life. I know I was not the perfect husband, but I believe you forgave my failings, as I did yours. Our love was not blind. It was compassionate, kind, and forgiving. I will forgive my imperfections and strive to improve. I will either move forward in this new, chaotic life, or I will deteriorate.

Logistics

L: There were plenty of loose strings to tie up after your death. At times, it was overwhelming. Maybe it was due to the quantity of tasks, but I think more so because doing anything requires so much more effort from the depths of grief. It's hard enough when things go smoothly but forget about it when you encounter obstacles. I felt my patience was especially thin as I worked my way through making all our affairs nicey nice.

I did not have a funeral or wake for you. If I had, I would have asked someone else to make all the arrangements. It would be an area prime for delegation. Even without having to coordinate an event, I still made two trips to the funeral home. Once to sign cremation paperwork and choose an urn, and later to pick-up your ashes. The process went quickly, but the funeral home was required to verify the cause of death with the county coroner before they could proceed. It took about two weeks to settle everything.

The funeral home notified the Social Security Administration of your death. I don't know if they're legally required to do this, but they did, and it was one less task for me. The home also obtained copies of your death certificate. As I learned in hindsight after my father died, it's better to ask for at least five originals. A few places will accept a copy, but most require an original.

Once the seriousness of your illness was apparent, you gave me a list of all your online accounts and passwords. This made many of my tasks easier.

I had to go slow, balancing the urgency of some items against the inertia it took to do anything. As C.S. Lewis recounted after his wife's death in *A Grief Observed*, "And no one ever told me about the laziness of grief…I loathe the slightest effort."

Notifications

Phone calls, emails, and letters to family and friends reporting your death. Your friend Joyce kept the peeps from your old workplace current on your status. I did not advise the post office of your death, so catalogs and ads addressed to you still arrive in our mailbox. I wrote "deceased, return to sender" on a couple, but for the most part they'll just stop sending stuff eventually. All the utilities—water, electricity, natural gas and garbage—were already under my name, so no action was required.

Health Insurance

Due to monthly premiums, canceling your health insurance was a priority. They changed their contact information about your account to me, necessary because the paperwork of medicine/insurance is often protracted. I continued to receive statements for at least six months after your death. I also notified our insurance broker so she'd know only I would require her advice next year.

Credit Cards

My experiences with our credit card vendors ranged from easy to contentious. In the aftermath, I advised every couple that would listen, to ensure each person was the primary card holder for at least one account. If you're secondary, the companies treat you as they would a stranger.

You had two cards. Banana Republic and Nordstrom. I simply closed the former, since I was not listed on the account, and even you only used it once a month or less. That was easy. A phone call. They took me at my word and didn't even require a copy of your death certificate as I recall.

The second card was the worst experience I had in this process. You (and in my mind, me by extension) had been loyal customers for decades. We both used the card as our main charge card and racked up over a thousand dollars a month. Unknown to their accounting department, it was me who wrote most of the checks to pay off the account balance month-after-month, for decades. When I asked them to make me the primary on the account, they told me I had to reapply as a new customer. I wasn't happy, but I did it. This required me to unfreeze my account at three credit bureaus for at least three weeks to allow enough time for them to receive and process my new customer application.

When I finally received my new card, it listed by credit limit at $300. I called again to correct what must be an obvious mistake. No, it wasn't. Why even bother? A monthly limit of $300 is useless. I told the customer service rep "This is bullshit."

That was the only expletive I used, but apparently it was enough to justify the rep being able to hang up on me. Fortunately, I'd told her to cancel the card before she hung up. I vowed never, under any circumstance, to ever shop there again. So much for customer service and loyalty.

Another effect on a card's authorized user (not the primary account holder), is a credit rating drop. This is another reason why it's better if both spouses establish at least one primary account of their own.

Newspapers

Our digital subscription to the *New York Times* was in your name. I went online under your account and made the changes. Our subscription to our local paper was already in my name, so I simply had to unsubscribe from their news updates that were sent to your email account.

Hospice Meds

There was cache of medicines left over after you died. Painkillers, tranqs, laxatives, and anti-nausea drugs. I bundled them up and took them to the pharmacy, depositing them in their metal lockbox. The hospice can't reuse any supplies that have been opened, so they picked up any that were intact when they came for all their equipment: hospital bed, wheelchair, walker, toilet chair, etc. The remaining supplies I either found a place to store or threw away.

Voter Rolls

A web search linked me to an election site for our county that included a downloadable form to report a deceased voter. I printed a copy of the one-page form, filled it out, and mailed it to the county Auditor's office via USPS.

Subscriptions

About six issues of *Real Simple* remained on your subscription, so I just let it run out. It was a favorite of yours. I browsed through the remaining issues as they arrived. It's filled with good advice on housekeeping and homemaking, but I don't have the same level of interest in these areas as you, so I didn't renew it.

All our subscriptions to streaming services had been in my name from the start, so there were no adjustments to make there. However, since I no longer spend my evenings with you watching TV, I canceled most of them and haven't looked back. I watch TV about an hour a night while I eat dinner. Afterward, I'm on my computer, my phone, listening to music, or reading.

Auto Insurance

After you died, I had three cars. I sold one after a month or so. A friend or ours who is a car aficionado, has bought and sold a lot of cars. He recommended several websites that buy direct and some that dealers use to source cars for their lots. Carvana gave me the best offer, so I went with them. I was surprised how relatively easy it was. I called our insurance company and had them remove your name from the policy and the third car. A month later they sent a refund check.

Phone Service

Like a certain credit card company, AT&T was not so easy to deal with. Our phones were under your account and AT&T would not simply reassign the account to me. If I hadn't had years of good service from them, I may not have stayed. I don't remember if they needed a copy of your death certificate to close your account. If so, a scan was probably acceptable. I had to reapply for my own account. As I remember, their process only required one of the major credit bureaus to verify my rating (despite being on your account for decades). The process was cumbersome and took a few weeks, but their reps were polite, and they offered the same level of support we'd had on your account, so

I stayed with them.

Credit Union

At some point along the way, we switched from a bank to a credit union, which generally offered better service. I went in person to the local office and had your name removed from our accounts. They required an original of your death certificate. I continued using our remaining checks, that included your name, until they ran out.

Retirement Accounts

I met with our financial advisor in a video conference to remove your name from our joint accounts and arrange to transfer the money in your IRA to mine. He handled all the hard stuff, sent me a variety of forms to sign, that I returned along with copies of your death certificate as needed. His work also included updating the beneficiary information on each account.

Taxes

I advised our tax preparer of your death. I still qualified to file jointly in the year that you died, but the next year I'll have to file singly and adjust the standard deduction downward. The change from we to me also means only one social security payment. This change happened the month after your death. Survivors can choose the higher of either spouse's payment, but going forward it'll be one instead of two, so it has a major financial impact.

Another penalty for being single will occur when/if I sell the house. While couples may exclude up to $500K of the sale price, singles are only eligible for half that amount. This is why we can't have nice things.

Computer/Phone

Thanks to your password list I had no problems logging into your accounts. Your web browser has many of them "memorized" so that was a good way to log into many of your favorite sites to make adjustments or close out your accounts. It's incredible how many companies we are connected to in this era.

Social Media

You were more active on social media prior to the pandemic, so you had more accounts than me. I debated a little about whether I should close the accounts. Harry, Whitney, and I all agreed I could leave them. It was the only way to connect with many of your peeps that I had no other way to reach, and it has been a bitter-but-sweet experience to review your old posts from time to time. In hindsight, I'm glad to have kept your accounts.

Email

You had dozens of vendors that sent you emails. I kept your email accounts and periodically unsubscribed to all of the vendors over time. In a few cases, I wrote to friends via your account to tell them the sad news of your death. Two years later, I still check your inbox from time to time to see if anyone requires a response.

Cards/Letters

Probably the last task directly related to your death was to reply to everyone who sent a card or email sharing their condolences and memories of your friendship. I took my time with these, writing one or two a day, until I finally had responded to everyone.

Ashes at Sea

I found only two charter services that offered ashes at sea charters in Oregon. The easiest to find was a long drive down the Oregon coast, but after scrolling deeper, I found Garibaldi Charters, who fit the bill. They are a seasonal service, operating over the warmest months when conditions are best. I made reservations for a June date in 2024.

One tip I picked up from somewhere (I've forgotten where) is that when friends offer support, categorize the kind of support you need so you can ask the right person:

Support Types

Listeners—people who focus on you. (Listeners, not advisors.)

Doers—people who can take on tasks to reduce your load.

Respite—people who can help provide a break from your grief, people who can distract you for a momentary respite.

Will

I know our Will includes "pre-deceased" language, so I haven't felt much urgency to have it updated, but it's something to address eventually.

Road Trip

L: You know our winters are relatively mild in the Pacific Northwest, but there is always the possibility of snow or ice a few times a year. If it snows, it usually gets packed on the road quickly and driving can be hazardous. Whenever it snowed, or threatened to snow, you stayed glued to the local news and your phone, constantly monitoring conditions. These were always times of high anxiety for everyone, but particularly stressful for you.

All wheel drive was not an option for Minis

when we bought the Mini Cooper Countryman in 2014, but in the years following I waited for an all-electric vehicle with AWD. Tesla had some, but they were out of our range. We waited and toughed out the winters until I spotted a VW coming to market that fit the bill. It also had a tight turning radius and good visibility—two other important criteria for us. I test drove the ID4 with you beside me, and we placed an order. Production was just ramping up. We expected a six-month wait, but it ended up being over a year. Our car was still in production when the dealer called reporting he had a car that met all of our specs except the color. It was deep red. Rather than wait another month or more for our original order, we opted to take it and drove it away in mid-July 2023. We took another test drive to refamiliarize ourselves with the car. It had more electronics than we were used to. I insisted you get behind the wheel this time just to be certain you liked it. It still makes me sad when I recall that this was the only time you ever drove our new car.

The large screen display for navigation was invaluable during your illness, as your medical appointments were numerous and often at places we'd never been before. The car was comfortable to ride in and easier to get in and out of than the Mini.

Small favors, but we were grateful.

We'd been driving an electric car for years, as our second set of wheels before the VW was an all-electric SmartCar, a two-seater that made the Mini look big. I loved the SmartCar, it was great as a commuter during my final work years. Its big drawback was its range, only 60 or 70 miles. The VW maxed out at 276. And, as the salesman at the dealership told us, you could easily take a road trip with it due to the expanding charging network built up over the past few years. We always charged the SmartCar at home, but the charging network was more important for a car with greater range.

After you died in mid-September, I felt the need to escape my new daily reality. Harry had a two-week vacation coming up in October. Whitney and Sean were living with us, so dog sitting was built in. I knew the Monterey Aquarium would be a big draw for Harry, and I suggested a road trip. I drove, but Harry was a big help in navigating and locating charging stations along our chosen route. It would also be a bonding opportunity for us and a welcome distraction from mourning.

One of my favorite Beatles tunes is *Two of Us*, from their final album. The line, "You and I have memories, longer than the road that stretches out ahead," came to mind in Monterey. You and I had been there long ago, before kids even. And much later, it was a highlight from our California road trip with Lucia.

Returning to a familiar place was a double-edged sword. It triggered my grief when I remembered our first visit to the aquarium, our walks in and around Monterey, and the magic of Carmel. But Harry and I explored different routes and stayed in a different place. It helped too, that a lot had changed over the years. In that way, we made new memories.

Therapists encourage those in grief to do new things, to make new memories, for their therapeutic value. Rather than going back to a favorite restaurant and feeling your conspicuous absence, therapists suggest trying a new restaurant and fostering new favorites. Make new memories. Prove to yourself you really are still here, and there really is more of life to explore. Take small steps. Go to a new coffee shop, have a cup, and leave. It doesn't have to be a big deal, but do it. In time, these small steps may lead to larger ones.

The road trip with Harry was good for both of us. The Monterey aquarium is one of the best in the world and Harry really enjoyed it. Since we visited on a Monday, during the school year, I'm sure there were far fewer people than on a weekend or some-time during the summer. The next day we walked about eight miles along the coastline in Pacific Grove. We ate lots of takeout food, and had room service one night to avoid restaurants, which Harry still felt uncomfortable with, post-pandemic.

I'm an introvert, but the open road has always appealed to me. It feels like an escape, and I really needed one following your death. I think Harry did too. I think I intuitively knew it would be renew-ing. We had a good time together, and we spent all of the week-plus inseparable. Our conversations ranged from light-hearted trivia to our struggles coping with grief. It was therapeutic, and by the time we got home, we were ready to return to the familiar but forever-changed home front.

I'm still here, and that fact is beginning to sink in. If there was some way to magically bring you back, I would want nothing more. I would much prefer to spend whatever time I have left with you. But that's not the choice. You're gone, and I remain. If you were here, if you were watching me from the afterlife, you'd want me to move forward. You would not want me grieving forever and moping around and feeling perpetually blue. You would want me to enjoy my remaining life. That is what

I've come to realize. I must move forward. I'll have to make decisions without your counsel or blessing. It'll be different, but I must learn to make solitary decisions and embrace them. I'll have to learn to push aside self-doubt and find solace in making a solitary life.

What'll I Do?

L: It's been about nine weeks since you died. I still miss you every day. My sadness comes and goes. Sometimes I have moments of joy when I think to myself, I am glad to still be here. This is new.

With all the kids in the house, our bedroom has become my retreat. I need a place for solace. I want to add a bookcase in a corner. This may not have been something you would've endorsed, but books bring me comfort, and I like being amidst them.

I remember early in our relationship we flew out to Portland from Madison to visit my sister. She worked nights, so we spent her days off together, but most days we were free to explore the city while she slept. We wandered through the shops in downtown, and uptown where she lived. We walked to Washington Park many times and laid in the grass, read, and swung on fifteen-foot-high swings. At night we bathed together in a clawfoot tub drinking wine by candlelight, listening to music, and making love.

One day we took a bus to Seattle and spent the day there, shopping and hanging out in Seattle Center, site of 1962's World's Fair. You looked so beautiful, I felt like the luckiest young man in the world to be loved by you. That summer held one of the best trips of my life.

So many years later, I remember looking at you at Whitney and Sean's wedding, still feeling so grateful for your love, and to have you in my life. You were such a beautiful person, inside and out. Having both of Sean's brothers there, with Harry performing the ceremony, was the best day of our final year together. I'm thankful there are so many photographs to remember the day.

Grief and I are well acquainted. I've begun re-reading *Why Me?* by Pesach Krauss and Morrie Goldfischer. I didn't recall much of it, but I remember it was very helpful when I read it 34 years ago after Colin died. The subtitle is "Coping with Grief, Loss, and Change." Now, I'm rediscovering its wisdom. Its advice is helpful in dealing with grief, but also for its insights into the rabbit hole of comparing yourself with others. We are all unique, and as affecting as praise or criticism from others can be, the only comparison that really matters is the one to yourself, along with your assessment of your potential. That's a lifelong lesson, and one I should remind myself of often.

I've felt a strong need for solitude, so I've begun walking every day again. It's a chance for me to be alone with my thoughts. Sometimes it's cold in Fall, but I wear gloves or a hat when necessary. It's the closest thing I do to meditation. There is traffic, but part of my two or three routes take me past fields and groves of trees. Seeing nature is calming and renewing. I need at least a daily dose of that right now.

Lucia texted about a week ago. Always good to hear from her. I guess it somehow makes me feel a little closer to you since you were best friends growing up—and I've known her as long as I've known you. I told her that you would want me to find a way to live without you; to grow and thrive, and all that. She agreed, that is what you would say if you were here. Her validation was comforting, particularly since she knew you so well.

A few days ago, I was invited to a party but declined. It's too hard for me to listen to minutia when my world has changed so profoundly. It wouldn't be fun. I feel hypersensitive about even the possibility of somebody saying something inappropriate or offering advice. C.S. Lewis wrote in *A Grief Observed*, "There is a sort of invisible blanket between the world and me. I find it hard to take in what anyone says."

When you're grieving, others may not know what to say. They may feel a past loss of theirs qualifies them to advise you. They may try to fix you, but you're not broken. You're in grief. To support someone in grief, ask them how they feel, how they're holding up. Ask them how their grief is progressing or changing. Grief is expressed with tears; feeling numb, hopeless, angry, guilty; and an inability to concentrate. You can ask about these things, and any other feelings their grief evokes. Ernest Hemingway said, "In our darkest moments, we don't need solutions or advice, what we yearn for is simply human connection—a quiet presence, a gentle touch." Aim for understanding and compassion. Don't make the mistake of trying to take on someone else's pain. Just listen, acknowledge, and be present.

In a group session on grief that I attended, the consensus was that those grieving want to be listened to, not lectured. When a friend has a story about the person who died, it can be the most comforting form of condolence. Another widow found joy when a stranger asked, "What was your husband like?"

I remember the Vice President of Marketing where I once worked approached me after Colin died. I'd worked in his department for over a year, but he'd never said a word to me in all that time. He told me I needed to be strong for you, that you really needed me now more than ever. I was polite and thanked him for his advice. As much as I may have wanted to be strong for you, after being devastated myself, the last thing in the world I felt was strength. I would be lucky to just survive the day, the week, the next year. Despite his lack of understanding, I gave him credit for approaching me and acknowledging Colin's death. He could've easily just ignored it.

Sometimes you read about people forgiving someone who has wronged them. The notable ones are like the woman who testifies at the trial of her rapist, and then says she forgives him. The experts advise that forgiveness frees the soul, so your offender no longer holds power over you. They categorize forgiveness as direct, indirect, and conditional. Direct means expressing your forgiveness in words or writing. Indirect is silent, where forgiveness is internalized. Conditional forgiveness requires the offender to acknowledge their offense, apologize, make amends, or promise not to repeat the behavior.

It helps to remember that people are at least partly a product of their environment. If they grew up in harsh conditions, it may be harder for them to act kindly. You can apply the same perspective whether you're trying to forgive someone else or yourself. Ultimately, it's about letting go instead of allowing some slight to eat away at you.

For me, it's easy to judge my feelings instead of simply recognizing them. Blaming myself can be as toxic as blaming someone else. I wish I had spent more time sitting with you on your final day. It's easy for me to feel guilty about this. Of course, I didn't know it was your final day, and I was obsessed with caring for you. At least I know that my behavior communicated how much you meant to me.

I can be my own worst critic. Now, when I feel guilty for one of my failings, I think about you. How would you judge me? Doubtless, with greater compassion than I typically judge myself. Just thinking about your kind heart makes me feel better.

With all my time alone, I've been thinking a lot about music lately. In particular, the song *What'll I Do*. Originally it was an oldie from our parent's generation, but the version I recall was Linda Ronstadt's from *What's New*, her first collaboration with Nelson Riddle. The song is really about a breakup, but most of the lyrics express the feelings of grief I feel so often. I don't know why I want to listen to songs that always make me cry, but I do. Maybe it's a way I use to face my grief. Maybe when tears well up in my eyes, and spill down my cheeks, they take a little bit of the day's sorrows with them.

There are plenty of days where the only thing I can tell you is that I'm still here. What does it even mean to be all right? My heart is broken. There's no balm for these feelings, nothing to do but endure. I retreat in distraction or avoidance at times. Grief demands it, or it will consume me. But it's only a much needed, momentary relief for the work of grieving. I think it's true: there is no way around it, you must eventually face it to learn to live with it. That means dwelling there and embracing the pain. It requires a push to delve into your memories and soak in your sorrow, but it's cathartic. A little weight is lifted after you release your emotions. Then I rest, until the next encounter.

NOKdoc

L: I never really thought that you would die before me. Statically, women live longer than men. You had a bad hip, but otherwise you were healthy, and you'd always eaten better than I did. Your diagnosis in August was shocking. The cancer was aggressive and swift. It spread so quickly our options crumbled one after the next. By September, all that was left was hospice. At least you spent your final week at home with your family.

I always believed I would die before you. Without a clue about life on my own, the shock of your death was compounded by my bewilderment at being alone.

None of our close couple friends have been split apart by death, and several are older than us. Your passing thrust home the reality of mortality. I was a dead man walking in the aftermath; brokenhearted, devastated, and numb. I knew there were things that needed attention, but motivation was difficult to muster. I found enough energy to address only a few tasks a day. After that I had to stop and sit quietly, or pace, or find a distraction of some kind.

It took a month or so to work through the loose ends that death leaves for the living. I had no sense of what's next—next week, next month, let alone next year. The only thing that felt important was to consider what I would leave behind for Harry and Whitney & Sean when I went. Many things were fresh in my mind, having just dealt with these things myself. My next task was to write a document that would help my kin sort things out after my death: a NOKdoc (Next of Kin document).

I wrote it over the period of a month or so, tackling different topics most days. This was the one project that broke through what was otherwise a lethargic daily routine after your death. I dated each topic so our kin would have an idea when each entry was current. [The topics are listed in the Appendix.]

I've done the best I can to ease the logistical tasks for Harry and Whitney & Sean when I'm gone. Beyond this I just have to let go. They'll handle things in their own way, finding their paths just as I do in this afterlife.

Therapy

L: Before you died, you made me promise I'd seek therapy to help me cope. Finding a therapist, or the right therapist, is more crucial than finding some other service provider, like a guy who fixes an oven, but it is sort of the same process. Unless you have a friend, who can make a recommendation, you're starting at square one.

I heard somewhere that the *Psychology Today* website was a great resource, so I started there. I specifically wanted a man, because I felt a man would have a greater understanding of what it means to lose a wife. There seemed to be a lot of good options, but as I got into the process, I discovered a lot of obstacles.

Because it's a much larger city, there are more therapists in Portland than Vancouver. That's fine until you realize that an Oregon therapist must be licensed to practice in Washington. I was expecting to meet online, but the border line still applies. Nearly all therapists offer an initial "get acquainted" session without obligation. I began contacting people and soon found similarities with other types of service providers. Many don't respond quickly, and some don't respond at all. Somehow, I thought therapists would be more responsive than an appliance repair service, but that was not the case.

I ended up saving my introductory email because I had to send it out so many times:

Dear _____,

My wife of 48 years died in September, and I am seek-ing advice on how to move forward. I am 70 and retired, so available most mornings. My location is Vancouver, Washington.

I would like an initial, online session to meet and dis-cuss how you could help, fees, and insurance coverage. My preferred contact method is email.

My insurance is _____. My understanding is that Medicare will cover Psychiatric Nurse Practitioners be-ginning in 2024.

Thank you for your time and consideration,

-Kenneth Richardson

I finally connected with someone in Portland who was also licensed for Washington. We talked about my situation via phone. I liked his demeanor. When we got into insurance, he told me Medicare would not cover therapists, only doctors like a Psy-chologist, which he wasn't. So, we had to part com-pany. He said he'd reach out to his network and see if he could find a potential lead for me.

He followed up through email about a week lat-er to report that he was not able to find anyone. He did however mention a therapist named David Kes-sler, who specialized in grief counseling through his website: grief.com. I'm indebted for his effort and support. He must be an amazing therapist; it's unfortunate I wasn't able to work with him.

An aside on therapy vs psychiatry: The tele-health service Doctor On Demand recommends therapy for anxiety, depression, relationship issues, stress, managing change, grief, and loss. They recommend psychiatry for feelings of being overwhelmed, emotions that disrupt daily living, managing medication, and family history of mental health issues.

I tried again to find a male psychologist on *Psychology Today*'s website and through my insurance company's referral search, but nothing really fit my requirements.

Providence hospice also provides counseling to family members of the deceased for up to a year. In fact, a woman called me to ask how I was doing a few weeks after you died. She was a good listener, but I could tell she was much younger than me and of course, she was a woman. She's no doubt a terrific therapist, but I couldn't really connect with her. I talked to her two or three times and then told her she didn't need to call again.

I'd also begun reading about grief, revisiting the two books that helped me the most when our son

Colin died, *When Bad Things Happen to Good People* by Rabbi Harold Kushner and *Why Me?* by Pesach Krauss and Morrie Goldfischer.

Tired of searching for a therapist, I decided to sign-up for David Kessler's online program Tender Hearts. The cost was $34/month, which I could afford without worrying about insurance negotiations. Considering an hour of therapy is typically $150, it sounded like a bargain. I could quit any time if it wasn't helpful. But it was. I've been a subscriber for many months. I've completed the program and still attend many of Kessler's special sessions with various grief experts and sometimes his regular group sessions where ordinary mourners check-in from around the country (or the English-speaking world) to share their status or ask for advice.

Much later, I learned of another online mental health care provider, Brightside Health. I have no experience with them, but I've made note of them for possible future use.

I'm sure a one-on-one experience with a therapist is different, but Kessler's approach has been helpful for me, helping me to understand more about this unwanted journey I must travel.

Finding the right resources wasn't a smooth

process, but your concern helped me persevere. Another symbol of our bond.

Grief left me reeling. It disrupted every balance there had been, and in some ways took control. When your birthday arrived less than two weeks after your death, I was frozen. I was able to honor your memory, but not much else. I felt much the same way about the first Thanksgiving without you. The less I did, the better. I learned later that this disorientation is common. It's part of grief, so I cut myself some slack.

Thanksgiving had always been a tough time of year for us. It was the time of Colin's birth and death. Our other children were grown by the time that I could truly embrace the holiday again as a day of celebration. For years our dinners were moderate affairs. Many years we ate out to minimize the cooking. In more recent years, you led the effort and expanded the number of side dishes and brought out the fine silverware we'd inherited from your mom.

For this first Thanksgiving without you, I simply ordered dinner from a deli. I reheated the precooked turkey and sides they provided. I knew this would probably be the last Thanksgiving meal at our house. The traditional celebration would move to Whitney and Sean's. Rather than lead the event, now I will simply be a participant—as it should be.

There can be a lot of expectations around holidays, but grieving takes precedent over tradition. I must dismiss expectations and assumptions, and do what feels best. For company, I choose friends or family that honor my grief. I could also cancel the holiday entirely if that's what felt best. I know my holidays will never be the same without you. At some point, I'll have to reinvent new versions.

Physical health is also under duress during grief. David Kessler hosted an online event with Mary-Frances O'Connor, author of *The Grieving Body* and *The Grieving Brain*. She said up to 80% of those grieving experience chest pain—literally an aching heart. Grief can also conjure up a sort of brain fog, making it more difficult to correlate physical issues (like back pain) to grief.

The presence of your love in my life helped diminish life's commonplace stressors. Now, that psychological balm is gone, so I must rely more on myself and others to counteract life's challenges. Intense grief affects hormones and the immune system which can increase the body's inflammation response, weaken the immune system, and even affect the natural aging process in seniors.

I'm told seeking therapy and staying on top of any physical issues is more important than ever when experiencing intense or protracted grief.

One of the topics explored in therapy is guilt or regrets I have about you. I wish I'd been a better listener. Maybe I'll be more mindful of listening in the future, I don't know. Another regret that gives me pause is your battle with hip/back pain. This went on for too long. You tried everything in the alternative medicine arena but never saw a doctor. Should I have pushed you harder? If you hadn't suffered chronic pain for so long, would it have altered your end-of-life journey? I don't wallow in these thoughts, because I know they aren't productive. But I do wonder at times if I let you down. There's no way to know for certain.

I mentioned this to my friend Jon who spent his career in medicine. He told me that throughout his years of experience with patients, you can only advise. You can't make anyone take your advice. He asked, "How many times have you brought prescription medicine home and then declined to actually take it?" Yes, I've done that more than once.

After Colin died, we tried again for a baby. When your pregnancy test was positive, we went in for the initial ultrasound. But the fetus had no heartbeat. I remember driving back home over the Willamette River and feeling anger more than any other emotion. Thinking we would face the same hardship as losing Colin was beyond comprehension. Fortunately, it was not the same sense of grief.

The doctor arranged to abort the fetus. Waiting to miscarry was dangerous and not recommended. I was at your side. You were conscious, but you hated the whole idea of it, and the anesthetic made you nauseous. You asked me to take you home, to stop this, and get you out of there. I felt awful. I so wanted to follow your desires, but the doctor insisted this was the best option for your health. I didn't stand in his way. You made it through, but I always felt this was my worst moment of betrayal to you.

We didn't talk about it once you were home, or even much later. Literally decades later, I think we were watching a documentary or a news report with a segment about a non-viable fetus. It highlighted all the dangers to the mother if an abortion was not performed. When you expressed relief that you'd had the procedure so long ago, you had no idea how good it was to hear you say those words. One of the biggest regrets of my life had been resolved by the most important person in my life.

Changes

L: Your death was, and is, still overwhelming me. Grief is exhausting, so any distraction can be welcome. Sometimes I distract myself with little, easy things like housework that offer a small feeling of having accomplished something. When I think of larger projects or changes, it's too much. I'll have to stick with the small stuff today and hope the motivation for something more important comes with time.

With Harry's help, I moved the desk you inherited from the living room into our bedroom—now, my bedroom. With all the kids here in the house, I needed a workspace for myself. These letters help me process my thoughts and emotions. Moving the desk is a small thing, but it feels strange to do it without any input or agreement from you. And there are things I imagine buying, like a dining room table. We agreed to replace the glass-top table we had for the last 30 years with a wooden one. Your death impresses upon me that we don't have forever. So, I'm shopping online for a table.

We had three cars. Or rather, I had three cars. That's ridiculous. I sold the Mini Cooper. It was the main car you drove, so emotionally it was hard to let go. But it was time. I'm sorry you only drove the VW once. I think you would've liked it and would have felt safer in a larger vehicle.

I drove Harry to and from work for two weeks and then asked him to use Lyft for the return trip at midnight. The returns were just too much for me—staying up late and driving at night on unlit highways, which I hate doing. There was no push-back; Harry understood that I just can't do it. Still, sometimes I feel as if I'm letting him down.

Would you approve of the choices, the decisions I make without you? Some yes, some I can't be certain of. Am I making changes that improve my life, or just distract me from my grief? I don't know. But I do understand that I can't move on without change. If only change didn't bring with it feelings of uncertainty and guilt. I suppose in time these feelings will fade, but for now they are real.

If the sum of the parts is greater than the individual pieces, then what am I without you? Less than us. There is a part of you that still lives inside me, but there is also a part of me that died with you. How do I go on as less than I was?

Grief is the first hurtle; fractured survival the second. "Who am I without you?" is the widower's dilemma.

Of the advice I've read online, the critical items for a healthy body are sleep, diet, and exercise. I've done great on the diet front. I am trying to sleep eight hours a night, but the dogs always wake me multiple times, and I often struggle to get back into a deep sleep. I suppose the light sleep I'm getting after midnight is still helpful, but I can't stop reliving your decline and death.

I read later, that after 70 sleep is often not as deep. I feel like my first session of about four hours is solid, but after my first trip to the bathroom, or Augie's midnight yard tour, my sleep is light. Sometimes it seems to shift back and forth from being awake and sleeping lightly. According to WebMD, I guess that's normal.

I'm still having a late afternoon cocktail every day after dropping Harry at work. Still wish I could resist. Everything I read advises against it, but that momentary reward/release is too seductive for me to forego.

I like writing to you. I can't talk with you anymore so maybe I'm writing a long, rambling love letter instead. Maybe this is one way to hold on to your spirit.

I brought out an electric candle that turns itself off after five hours. It's on the windowsill in our room, and it lights every night. This ritual has become important to me, like putting on my wedding ring every morning. How long does one wear his wedding ring? What will it mean if or when I stop? Will it signal moving on or a betrayal of your memory?

Motivation is hard to find these days, so it seems like a good idea to seize any motivation that happens to surface.

We've always done upgrades to our living spaces. Sometimes big things, like a remodel, but more often smaller things like a new rug or bedside table. We tended to go slow and get to things in our own sweet time. You were always tapped into the design and decorating world, finding things that would best serve our needs and aesthetics.

If there is anything that motivates me now, it's the desire to "finish" what we started. I found a dining room table that checks all my boxes. I hope you would've liked it. And so, I move forward on my own, hoping my choice complements yours and doesn't clash with the style you worked so hard to achieve.

There is an illogical sense of guilt about making these decisions without you, as if I'm purposely ignoring your input. Would you approve of my choices and their costs? I can only try, but I'm on my own. I can only lean on whatever you taught me in these areas where your strengths far exceeded mine. Just another of the many ways in which your absence is so sorely felt.

I've always liked a big house, but without you, this place may be too much. There's a lot to maintain for just Harry and me. And when I'm gone, it's hard to imagine him here all by himself. I took a looksee at Redfin today, just to see what's out there in condos and townhouses. When I asked Harry what he thought about moving, I was thinking of somewhere closer to his work, but he surprised me by saying he preferred Vancouver to Portland.

As I've perused Redfin, finding a condo with a small backyard space is not very common. But I can't picture myself taking Augie outside four or five times a day in a high-rise. I'll still browse Redfin from time to time, but I think we'll stay here as long as Augie is around. At that point, I will likely be tired of yard work and be ready to downsize. When I'm gone, a condo would be much better for Harry.

Like with housework, I'm trying to streamline yard work as much as possible. I heard good things about a landscape designer who did some work for one of Whitney's friends, so I hired her to work up a design to simplify the front and back. It's not money I really want to spend, but at my age I just have to bite the bullet and hire this out. Hopefully, the changes will increase the house's value to some extent and can at least be partially recouped when I eventually sell it.

A homework question from Kessler's Tender Hearts program was: What value can I find in my [grief] journey?

To respond, I have to contextualize and face the fact that death is inevitable. One of the two of us had to go first. With that reality, I can dig for some value. I think I'm less fearful of death now. When I die, I'll be losing myself, but not you. I'm also more conscious of how fragile life is. I have a better understanding of how devastating the death of a spouse is. I'm less self-critical of my decisions/failures; for most things, the stakes just aren't that important.

Someday, I hope to feel more gratitude for the time I had with you, than grief over the time without you.

Deafening Silence

L: Yes, it's quieter in the house without you, but

with Harry, Whitney & Sean, and two dogs, it ain't that quiet. For me, where the silence is most deafening is online. Every time my phone pings announcing the arrival of a text, I think of you and my hopes are dashed because of course, it can't be you, you're gone. This reaction persisted for far longer than I would have expected, but it's a common phenomenon among the bereaved.

There's a song about loss called "Let Go" sung by Allison Moorer. In one verse she laments expecting a call, even knowing it will never come. She just can't help holding onto the hope for things to be as they once were—even knowing they won't, she can't let go.

I'm afraid social media is the same. I was fairly active on several platforms prior to your death. I made posts to promote my projects, but also for friends and family. And of course, I followed you and always looked forward to your thoughts, your photography, your artwork, your kindness, and humor. Now, the silence is deafening. Social media is far less rewarding without you.

Since you died, my projects have waned. I have less to post about, and less interest to post at all. I've also soured on supporting the world's billionaire class, so although I keep my accounts, my engagement is far less than it was in the before times.

I looked over your password list one day, and after far too long a time, posted a message to your friends using your FB account. The replies were compassionate and validated again how much you were loved by so many of the people who knew you. I talked about whether I should close the accounts with Harry and Whitney. In the end, I decided to leave them online. I suppose the hosts will someday close them after years of inactivity, but for now I sometimes like to go back and scroll through your old posts. It's a unique sort of photo album of better times.

I've done the same with your email accounts—kept them. I unsubscribed from all the newsletters, vendors, and elected officials who sent you updates. What remains are a few old personal emails. Someday I may copy those worth keeping, and then perhaps close the accounts for good. Your contacts list was also helpful at times because it contained people I wouldn't have otherwise been able to reach.

L, my seventieth birthday arrived exactly three months after your death. Normally, a milestone birthday like this comes with a combination of dread, for breaching another decade; and celebration, for reaching the milestone. After retirement, there don't seem to be any more important age milestones. Maybe a better mindset is after retirement every age is an important milestone. But on my seventieth, I didn't think much about my entry into a new decade. According to some studies I've read about online, at a certain age (as in seniors) when a spouse dies, there is a 60% chance the other will follow within three months. Shocking, I know. So, I made it three months without you. I still grieve every day, but I'm not ready to join you just yet.

Everything Reminds Me of You

L: Early in our working lives, I did a fair amount of freelance graphics work on the side. I named the company Lark Design, after us. Years later when I started publishing, I wanted to use Lark Press. But this was now the internet era, and everything revolves around what URL is available. Every combination of Lark with Press, Books, Publishing, etc. was already taken. So, it became Larque Press. But like the original, it's still a tribute to our relationship.

Triggers spark memories. They can be welcome or unwelcome. The tough ones are unexpected and surface suddenly. Sometimes I'll be driving and see long gray hair trailing down the back of a woman walking down the street, and I'll think of you. How I wish I could run my fingers through your hair again, but I need to keep my mind on driving.

Another trigger for me is hospitals. We drove to so many medical facilities around Vancouver and Portland in the space of a month I don't even remember all of them. But later, when something else brings me by one, a flood of emotion rises.

Even welcome triggers can be unexpected. When they're planned, they're better described as tributes or memorials. I read about a widower who placed a picture of his wife in every room in his house, so he would always be reminded of her no matter where he went. An inspiring act, and one I adapted in my own way. Shortly after you died, I found a favorite picture of you at the goat farm we visited with Whitney a few years back and made it the home screen on my phone. I found a beautiful selfie you'd shot, printed a color 5"x7," and put it in a frame on my desk in our room. It's turned so I can see you as I sit in bed every morning and every night.

Every room in our house has reminders of you and our lives together. Some have always been there, and others are things I've taken from storage and added to the room's decor. The painting of you as a child that your grandmother crafted on a little ceramic plate. The etching of a sleeping camper with her dog by Laura Brusselaers from Estonia that I gave you for your final birthday, long before we knew it would be your last. You loved it; we both shed a tear when you unwrapped it and saw it for the first time. Now, it holds even greater meaning for me. And your artwork; all the paintings and drawings I've found are displayed throughout the house.

Favorite items of yours like little boxes or figurines, objects of that ilk that we bought together during our shared lives, even utilitarian things like quilts, armchairs, silverware, and so many others—they all remind me of you. They are simply things, but they are part of the fabric of two lives entwined together for over 50 years. They are simply things, but they bring me comfort when loneliness rises up. Everything here reminds me of you, and within each a tiny spark of you remains.

C.S. Lewis wrote: "Her absence is like the sky, spread over everything."

Life Lessened

L: Why do I feel so sad and blue tonight? I'm reminded again of how different everything is without you. It's not as good. I feel very alone to-night. I'm missing you so, it almost feels physical. During my mid-night awake period I felt that hole in my heart again. As my fitful night went on, my thoughts drifted to an upcoming appointment. I got angry at the seemingly endless dentist visits of the past few years. Is it aging, broken down teeth, or exploitation by greedy dentists? I don't know, and you're not here to talk about it.

Once I fell in love with you, I wanted to be with you constantly. Every moment I was alone, I missed you. I still did things on my own, but everything I did with you was better for it. Over time, my in-dependence grew more balanced, but my feeling of completeness and comfort when I was with you also grew. With you everything was better. The best of life's highs were more wonderful when you were by my side. Even life's lows—little and major—were always made more bearable, made better by your presence.

Now that you're gone, everything is less. The highs aren't as high, and the lows are lower. I don't know if that will ever change. Maybe time will tem-per the contrast, maybe not. Your absence is palpa-ble so much of the time.

Day By Day

L: A flurry of emotions riddles me now that it's been six months since you died. It seems impossible. Of course, time moves in a smooth, continuous progression. I know that. But it feels both sluggish and swift. I've made so little progress and yet six months have evaporated. Every morning, I take my vitamins and supplements. I've come to think of them like Patty Griffin's bitter pills in her song "Useless Desires." All I can do is maintain and eke out a flimsy satisfaction from whatever tiny victories I can claim by day's end.

I experience this passage of time that feels fast and slow simultaneously, again and again. The Wordle puzzle accrues your wins. Sometimes it makes me sad to see another 50+ day streak. I record my daily tasks in a little notebook. It's unsettling when all the pages are filled, and I must start a new one.

How can it be that so much time has vanished? I don't feel so much better. The experts will tell you that early grief is two years. Six months in, I believe it. I can't see the light ahead. I can only trust in the process; and trust I will someday feel more love than sorrow.

We went through this together with Colin. And although I don't remember the timeline, eventually we each came to live with the loss. Then too, we only knew him for nine months leading up to his birth, compared to the 50 years that I've been in love with you.

I know I should focus on those 50 years. I should celebrate all the time I knew and loved you. The greatest privilege of my life. I hope I'll get there in time. Right now, I'm sad and blue, and take each moment as it comes. But I'll keep the faith. Every day survived is progress.

Writing to you about my journey through this valley helps me work through my sorrow. My victories seem small, but writing helps reinforce whatever positives I manage to find.

Pressure Points

L: Some people have a lot of anger in grief. More so, if it was modeled for you in childhood. My grief makes it harder than ever for me to have patience when something doesn't go smoothly, like when an unexpected obstacle suddenly appears. That's when I get angry.

We had ants in the house again this spring. It's normal, and usually fairly easy to deal with, but this year it made me angry. Not much later I found signs of mice in the garage. I dealt with that too, but it upset me. Maybe I have repressed anger over your death. It was so unfair. Maybe I haven't really come to grips with that sense of injustice.

The thieves of balance are everywhere. The experts advise some scammers study the obituaries for opportunities to prey on the newly widowed. I know when I was most overwhelmed during the first few months of sorrow, I would have made an easier target.

Beware: the same sort of caution may be necessary if an obituary includes the time and place of services. The experts suggest arranging for a house sitter during services, since your home might be a theft target during that publicized time.

Wedding Ring

L: I wore my wedding ring every day for about six months. Putting it on in the morning felt like solidarity, like honoring your memory. But after a time, I started to wonder what friends would think. Would they see it as tribute or denial? This conflict would be amplified by anyone I met who later learned you'd died. I tried wearing the ring on my right hand, but that ring finger is slighter fatter, and it was difficult to remove unless greased with soap. I finally decided to stop wearing it. I am a widower, whether I like it or not—and I don't. Now, on special occasions like your birthday, Mother's Day, or other holidays, I slip it on in your honor. Likewise, I often wear one of your T-shirts on those days; even if it's under a long-sleeved shirt when it's cold. It brings me a small measure of comfort. Like a secret love that will never die.

You were always so loving, I know you'd support whatever I decide about wearing my wedding ring. In the end, my choice to go without is to help face the fact that you're gone. With or without the ring, you remain in my heart every day.

Medical Bills

L: You were always frugal, so you'd be pleased to know your medical bills were modest. Thankfully, your insurance bore the brunt of the bills. It would have been different if there had been treatments, or the illness had gone on for months or years. But your cancer was so aggressive the timeline from your first doctor's visit to your death was only a month, including the 12 days of hospice care.

The bills also include 12 or 13 days in a hospital, either PeaceHealth and Providence. Your insurance sent statements for all the expenses from August 18 to September 18, but the updates continued until May 2024, eight months after your death. I've done a quick tally to add up everything without doing a line-by-line, month-to-month comparison. The total from the medical providers was $230K. Of this the insurance agreed to pay $45K and left $2.5K for us. Transparent to me were the hospice bills. They dealt directly with the insurance, and I never saw the charges. There was also a lab cost for a DNA analysis (CDx) that cost $6K, but the lab forgave the debt because the work was done on October 10, and you'd died on September 18. The lab order should have been canceled, but that communication never happened.

For all the complaints people have about medicine and insurance—and at times I'm among them—I have to say this aspect of your demise was the least of my worries. I have nothing but gratitude for all the nurses and doctors and orderlies you saw during your journey, with special thanks to Providence Hospice. Their counsel and compassion helped us all.

On our first Mother's Day without you. Whitney wrote, "I had a feeling like suddenly waking up from a dream. I felt the weight of your death.

The pain and unfairness of it all was so sharp. I was overwhelmed with the feeling that all this life that had happened since you died showed up late. Like all this life we are living now has missed the main event. There's all this space left by your not being here, and it makes some days feel especially hollow.

"On May 31, 2024, we told Dad and Harry that Sean and I were going to have a baby. I wish so badly that you could be with us to meet this new person."

Months Nine to Sixteen
Handling Your Cremains

L: Your death forced a massive, unwanted change in my life. Your cancer and decline were entirely beyond my control. I think this feeling of helplessness drove me to want to control things in the aftermath. I think that desire to control something contributed to my lack of patience whenever even minor obstacles arose. In time, my equilibrium has returned to a better balance. My only real control is over myself.

I remember reading years ago about the circle of influence. When I put my attention on things within my control, my circle of influence expands. When I focus on things I can't control, my circle of influence contracts. Focusing on things like assumptions, expectations, comparisons, what-ifs, victimization, and projections aren't helpful. I can't change the weather. I can only note the forecast and plan accordingly, knowing that the forecast is just an informed possibility.

I picked up your ashes months ago. They were packaged in a heavy plastic bag, tucked into a black box with a lid. This was the most basic container. I didn't want a fancy urn because I knew your ashes were destined for the ocean. I had the box out on a bookcase in our room for a week or two. But seeing it was uncomfortable. It wasn't like a photograph of you, it felt like a stark reminder you were dead, every time I saw it. I moved it into your closet.

As the dispersal date approached, I started thinking about how things were going to work. I found an assortment of heavy cardboard tubes designed for cremains dispersal online and ordered one. When it arrived, it included instructions on how it worked. They were pretty good, but I found a video online that was even better.

I was nervous about transferring your ashes from the plastic bag into the tube. Fortunately, your ashes were more granular than powdery. I was able to pour them all into the tube with no visible residue stuck to the sides of the plastic bag, and no cloud of dust rising into the air. I breathed a sigh of relief, closed up the tube as directed, and placed it back in the closet.

During the dispersal, all of your cremains were released as planned, following the procedure noted in the instructions. No residue remained in the cardboard tube. I bought it back and disposed of it when we got home.

The Last Time

L: Reminders of your absence are constant. Some are expected, like going to bed alone, or ordering take-out for one instead of two. But there are so many things I never considered or expected that suddenly remind me that you're gone. They lessen over time, but then seemingly out of the blue, another rises up to confirm my harsh new reality.

Early on, what a strange feeling to wash your final load of laundry. Every step of the process—wash, dry, fold—was a haunting reminder you're gone.

For the first time, in this final house together, we each had our own sink in the primary bathroom. So, where we'd formerly shared a tube of toothpaste, here we each had our own. Yours was left for me to finish. That last bit of your toothpaste was another reminder the past is gone. A place I can't dwell, because I can't live there. Another reminder of my new reality.

When I was cleaning out your vanity I paused over your hairbrush. Long grey hairs had collected in the bristles. I hesitated for a moment. Maybe I should keep them in an envelope, but no, I couldn't be that sentimental about them. On occasion I have since thought of finding a cache of your hairs somewhere else as I slowly work my way through old possessions. Still, I don't regret the decision to discard them. Your mom kept a lock of your childhood hair, and I remember you thought it was kind of odd. Like a symbol of a past reality that no longer existed. You were right.

Sorting through your purse and wallet, I collected your driver's license, insurance cards, and in a drawer somewhere, your passport. I still have them, but they aren't much different than a lock of hair.

We shared our subscription to the *New York Times*, and we both loved to work The Mini crossword every day. We did it independent of each other. I usually went first, and when I was done, I cleared it, so you'd have a clean slate when you got to it. After you died, there was no longer any reason for me to clear it. I kept on doing the puzzle, but for months every time I finished a pang of loneliness struck as I wrestled with the end. Should I clear it as I always did, or leave it because it no longer mattered? It took me months to let go of a habit that was once second nature.

It's not unexpected that mail continues to arrive addressed to you. Most of it consists of catalogs and junk mail. As the months accrue it becomes a little less frequent and can sometimes be jarring when suddenly there's something for you again after so long.

Another hard one, was the day when I had to reorder our checks. Suddenly, your name had to be stricken from the address. Another grim erasure of your existence. The sadness and guilt returned when I wrote the final check with both our names.

These moments of the final time—or the first time without—are less frequent as time goes by. But I know something unexpected can arise to remind me this journey is a long, solitary road.

In June 2024, Whitney planted the zinnia seeds she'd collected from your flower bed. A few days later we took a walk together. We talked about you and the gestating baby, and baby names. Your go-to baby name was "Little Apple." We could only wonder what other baby names you would have suggested.

Whitney also had a dream about you. She recalled, "I was at a birthday dinner at our old house in Vancouver and both you and Dad were there. You had gotten some kind of pass to come back and spend the day with us, and you wanted to know how some things turned out since you were away. I can't remember exactly what you asked about. I let you know it all worked out, that we were able to take care of ourselves and each other. You seemed relieved to know we were doing well. When the night was over Dad gathered the coats and your periwinkle blue sun hat. I asked Dad where you were, and he said you weren't here anymore. Then I remembered you were gone and woke up crying. It hurt to wake up, but it felt so good to see you, and I remember longing to have another dream like that."

Ashes At Sea

L: The phrase "Ashes at Sea" appeals to me in many ways, and I know the idea that our remains are reunited with nature via the ocean resonates with you. In this way, your ashes are reunited with Colin's. "At Sea" also captures how I feel—intensely early on—less often now, but still profoundly; I am at sea without you. I guess I will always be at times until, at last, I join you.

Since we dispersed Colin's ashes at Ecola Beach in the city of Cannon Beach, I wanted you near him.

On May 6, 1989, we simply waded into the ocean and said our final farewells.

Over the preceding days—or perhaps weeks—I wrote Colin's eulogy. I wept every time I revised and polished it until it expressed the feelings in my heart. I had never written anything as powerful, and it inspired me to dare to pursue writing as a career. For that, I credit Colin. One of the many gifts he brought during his short, short time on this Earth. Whenever I write, it's one way in which I honor his memory.

Colin

It's hard to say goodbye to you.
I want to tell you how sorry I am for all your pain.
And for all of life that you will never know,
At the same time, I want to remember you with love,
Not your pain and our sorrow.

The first time I saw you I knew you were my son.
It was wonderful, for a brief, precious moment,
To take you in without fear.
After all those months of thinking about you,

Planning for you and waiting for your arrival.
It was wonderful to meet you.
You made us very proud and happy.

We all wonder what our lives mean.
Your life was very special to us.
And when you died, a part of each of us died too.
Your Mom and I think about you every day.
And your Grandma and Grandpa and Louise and
So many, many people's lives were touched by yours.
Your life had such great meaning.
You left many gifts for us with your passing.
You taught us how precious a gift life is.
You taught me how to grieve and
how to find light in sorrow.
And the love you made, the love that we have for you,
Will last our lifetimes.

Goodbye Colin, our son, our brother, goodbye.

In Oregon, ashes at sea are legal anywhere along the coast, at least three miles away from shore. There aren't many charter outfits that offer this service. None in Cannon Beach, but there is one a short distance down the coast in Garibaldi. I made the arrangements for June 20, 2024. We had to wait until the summer season when the ocean is calmer and the temperature a bit warmer.

I worked on your eulogy in the months between, rewriting and changing directions more than once.

Sean volunteered to drive Harry, Whitney, and I to Garibaldi. Whitney arranged for a friend to stay with the dogs at our house; ours, Augie, and Whitney and Sean's, Summer. We could have left the dogs alone, but we'd be gone most of the day, so the dog sitting help was a blessing.

You and I wanted your cremains scattered at sea. The winds at sea would be strong and gusty, but the ash container I bought was well designed and should work perfectly.

I bought a new, black shirt for the voyage, but dressed in layers like everyone else. Temperatures can vary quite a bit between shore and three miles out on the ocean.

We followed the map app to the dock in Garibaldi and parked in a large, ramshackle public lot and walked down to the dock area. There were numerous piers, slips, and lots of boats, none with obvious markings. We explored the area and searched for numbers to identify our charter but couldn't find it. I walked West downhill to a building that housed a charter company. It wasn't ours, but I thought they might point me in the right direction.

A kind soul there went out of his way to help. He not only knew the dock, he actually walked with me back to our little group and showed us exactly where to go. He must've noted our black shirts and offered a few words of advice. "Place the wind at your back when you release ashes." Then he looked me in the eye and promised us something magical would happen. That seemed hard to imagine under the circumstances, but I was grateful for his kindness.

The coast was foggy, with light winds. After the crew finished prepping the boat, we boarded. It could hold up to 20 people, but I didn't invite anyone outside our immediate family. I didn't want to share our farewell, and I also didn't want to coordinate more people. I came to understand the roots of these feelings a few months later, but I'll tell you more about that in another letter.

Most often the boat was used for fishing. For our ashes at sea, it was simply the captain and one crew member, Mate Tuck. As we got underway, Captain Dewey went over the safety rules and said he'd announce when we'd reached the spot three miles out. Then he'd power down the engines as low as possible but still be moving forward. We could take as much time as we needed and simply had to let him know when we were ready to head back.

It was cold, and although the sea wasn't particularly rough, the waves still managed to breach the deck from time to time, so we stayed inside the main cabin until we reached our destination.

In the days preceding this one—and while we rode out the roiling waters—the words to the song "Useless Desires" played out in my mind over and over. In particular, the lines "Goodbye, goodbye, goodbye, old friend. You won't be seeing me again." I hoped we'd meet again one day in the afterlife, but I have to accept it's more likely we won't. This haunting refrain expressed the truth of the moment.

It was hard to walk around the ship while at sea. You had to hang on to something with every step, preferably with both hands. When the boat powered down, we made our way outside to the aft deck. We sat on a wide bench and each of us shared our farewells.

Harry has a remarkable memory. He can remember details of events or dialogue from TV shows he watched ten years ago. He told me later his thoughts leading up to this day had drifted back again and again to that day he waited alone on the beach, a week shy of 26 months old, as we bid farewell to Colin. Of course, he didn't understand what we were doing at the time, but it must surely be one of his earliest memories.

Harry can always make you laugh with a wry observation or retelling a gag from a sitcom or podcast, so in his final adieu he recalled a few lines from George Constanza about the angry sea; because he knew how much you loved *Seinfeld*.

A few days earlier, Whitney had spent the whole day on Father's Day, June 15th, with me, talking while we assembled a jigsaw puzzle. When Harry and Sean joined us later, we watched *The Lords of Flatbush*, and ate no salt/low sugar, almond fig cupcakes that Whitney made for the occasion.

Here's what she wrote in her diary about the 20th:

"I remember the boat rocked more than I expected, and I was glad I had taken the Dramamine. I remember we saw a bunch of pelicans flying alongside the boat—they were probably looking for fish, but it felt special to see so many and be out at sea with them. I remember the farther we went from shore, the more clouds there were, and the more choppy the water was. I remember when we couldn't see land anymore, everything looked stormy and grey, and it felt like we were in another world. I don't

think I've ever been that far out on the ocean before.

"When it was time to say something, I read 'When Great Trees Fall' by Maya Angelou. *I felt like I needed her words to help give my feelings a way to come out. I remember feeling like I couldn't find words for everything on my own. In the poem, Angelou talks about a great tree that falls, and leaves this haunting quiet, and this scary, painful space that causes the life around the tree to shrink back and fall into shock. She talks about how, after a time, that shock dissipates a little and we can remember that the tree existed, and how we can carry its greatness with us as we continue to be.*

"I like those words because I feel so shaped by Mom, I see her in the things, thoughts, and experiences around me every day. I like the idea that her greatness in my life can continue with me.

"I know I was pregnant with Ann then, but I can't remember if I said anything about her. I think at that point I still felt scared something would happen to her. I also think it was as hard then, as it is now, to think of myself as a mother, when for my whole life that title has only meant my mom. I hope I can honor her by sharing the magic she brought to my childhood with my own daughter.

"I remember when my dad poured Mom's ashes out into the ocean, I felt a small amount of peace. Before that

moment I was afraid I would feel panic at seeing this tangible part of her falling away from us and out of reach. I worried it would feel like losing her all over again. Instead, for me, I think it felt more like this physical piece of her was now released and free in the universe. Like she was back in this primordial place where life originated, ready to continue on in this new way."

Sean spoke next. He told me later that he struggled getting his feelings into words. In fact, what he'd originally written was abandoned in the moment. Instead, he said he felt you were an exceptional woman who went out of your way to make sure other people felt welcome in your home and family. You always tried to bring joy to others. The world was worse off for not having you in it.

I had warned everyone upfront, I might not be able to read my eulogy aloud and after the first sentence my voice faltered, and I had to read the words to you silently, while everyone patiently waited for me to finish.

My sweet baby. Here we are, forced apart again, nine months after they took you away to the funeral home. I've been at sea ever since, just like now. I still wonder how I'll get along without you. The valley of sorrow is wide and deep, like an ocean. There are no detours, just one step, one moment at a time, hoping there's a way out someday. You and I have been here before, when Colin died. So, I know there is a life after eventually. As hard as that was 36 years ago, in its own way this is worse, because you are not here to share the sorrow. And I am so much closer to my own end. At least now your ashes and Colin's will reunite. I hope your spirits have already.

When I fell for you so long ago, I fell for a lifetime. No looking back, soaring like the ravens you loved. You were magical. You were my angel, my touchstone, my soulmate. You gave me the best years of your life, and the best years of mine. Now, my heart is broken. You held so much of it within yours. And when you died, my heart broke in two, and half stayed with you. But love is shared. What's left of me in this life, still holds tight to a part of you. I hope you know how much you were loved—by me, our children, and those close to you.

I want to believe your spirit still lives on out there somewhere, so we can be together again someday. So, I will say farewell, not good-bye. Farewell, my sweet angel, my sweet love. I will love you for as long as my spirit lives.

I needed both hands to release your ashes from the scattering urn, so I couldn't hold onto the rail to steady myself as the sea churned under our feet. Harry and Whitney hung onto my arms to steady me while I leaned over the rail. That felt right, cementing our unity in the moment.

I opened the tab of the urn and your ashes spilled out into the roiling waters below, briefly visible until the waves engulfed them and swept them from our sight. I think we all felt a moment of release and symbolic closure in this act. For Harry, it was even more intense. He felt that magic moment our kind-hearted friend on the dock had promised.

We made our way, grasping rails and handholds back to the cabin. I told the captain we were ready to return, and he sped up the engines and made for shore.

The sky had remained grey with clouds throughout the journey, but as we neared the port, they parted revealing the beautiful, blue Oregon sky. Being at sea, far enough out so there is nothing but water on the horizon is a bit surreal. Like soaring aloft in an airplane, you place your fate in the hands of those who built the craft and the crew who guide it. There is a natural, emotional response to the first sight of land after nothing but water. Add the sunshine and the steady calming of the water, and you can't help but feel a sense of relief. But the feeling was greater than the sum of those parts. Scattering your cremains was a milestone in our grief journeys, and the welcome sunny shoreline was a glimpse of a life ahead, a moment of elation, that there could be sunshine again, somewhere down the road. That was my magic moment. A promise kept.

Before I left the boat, I thanked Captain Dewey, expressing my gratitude for offering this service. He handed me a condolence card that included the position of your ashes:

N 45 34.757

W 123 59.917

Before our journey, I posted a note on your Facebook page and asked friends to remember you on this day. Many shared their thoughts and love.

My reply: "If you took a moment to think of L on that day I'm grateful—we're grateful. And I know her spirit is as well.

"The things that matter in this life are simple. And with a nod to Ringo, choose peace and love, and you'll never go wrong."

Regrets

L: A common emotion in bereavement is regret. Now that you're gone, what would I do differently if I could somehow relive our lives together? I would talk less and listen more. Your approval meant so much to me, I was always trying to impress you with what I knew or thought. In hindsight, I wish I had calmed down a bit and asked more about what you thought about things. For that, I am truly sorry.

When you entered hospice, we knew your days were numbered. I wish I'd asked the nurses about the signs of impending death that I later gleaned from presentations given by hospice nurses and from books. If I had been more prepared, I would have spent more time sitting with you and holding your hand in your final days instead of focusing so much on caretaking tasks. I regret it, but I have come to terms with it.

I was never perfect. You knew my flaws better than anyone, and you still loved me; I believe with all your heart. Your love absolved me, even of my shortcomings on your final journey through hospice. I'm certain you knew how much you meant to me from our heady days of first falling in love until the very end of our lives together.

One of my homework exercises from Tender Hearts was to write a letter to you about forgiveness:

L,

We were both human, both imperfect, but I don't think our shortcomings were often, if ever, left hanging.

Our love was always strong; tested at times but never lost. Forgiveness and kindness were always close-by, and conflicts reconciled in short order.

If I'm denying some secret or hidden hurt, I forgive you for it. If you harbored some unspoken regret or injury that I caused you, please forgive me. Our love is all that matters. Even now, ten months after your death, you will always be the greatest love, the greatest friend I ever knew.

I don't know if you can hear me. If you can, you know it's true. If there is only emptiness after death, I hope, and I want to believe, you knew how much you were loved by me, Harry, and Whitney, and by Sean, our friends, and all of your friends like Joyce and Craig. You made everyone's time in your presence better.

With all my love,

–Ken

An Amendment to Forever

L: Growing up I learned the concept of forever from music, fiction, and film. "I will love you forever!" is declared as the gold standard of love. We are enamored with the idea of infinity, that life's most important aspects are everlasting. Our earliest stories taught us the good people of the world will live happily ever after.

No wonder we're incapable of grasping forever. No wonder we're out of touch with our mortality. How can you cherish every waking day, when your mindset expects your life will simply go on and on? The universe may go on forever. Time may continue forever, but we can't truly understand what this means. Although the intent of forever love is meant to be the greatest gift one can give, it's a bit grandiose. "I will love you as long as I live," is more accurate and, let's face it, more possible.

So, that's it. I will love you, L, as long as I live. I've told you many times in words and in ways while you were here with me. And I still feel it, I still feel you, right now, even though you're gone. As long as I live, you will live in my heart, because I love you as I have loved no other.

It's now been 11 months without you. I still get sad. I still miss you multiple times every day. But I have come to accept that you're gone, and I'm less certain your soul is still out there. I can still feel your presence at times, but these are more like memories or tributes. When I make decisions now, I'm less likely to think about whether you would approve or not. Now, it seems moot. I'm still here and I must make decisions without you—and then live with them.

Awake Mid-Night

L: I only seem able to sleep well about every other night. Augie doggie doesn't help. I treasure his companionship, but he always wakes me up mid-night, just like a little champion. So, I often have trouble getting back to sleep. That's when I dwell on the past, often the recent past. The doctor visits, the bad news, and your suffering. My regrets about not being perfect, more attentive during our final years together. It's like doomscrolling. When it becomes unbearable, the only way to break the spell is to get up. So, I make a pot of half-caf and sit in bed reading the *Times* on my phone. If I'm still not tired after that, I start on the puzzles.

Sometimes when I think about losing you and losing others in our lives, I wonder who's next? Probably not a healthy place to dwell, but I think it's natural to pause there for a bit. The price of love is loss, but I can't see allowing the risk to stop me from ever loving again. Before too much longer my granddaughter will arrive, and already she has my heart. Whatever time that remains for me, I hope it's filled with love.

What if I'm the next to die? There's no way to tell. Today, I want to go on as long as I can. But I can only take care of myself and hope for the best.

I wonder sometimes if I've hit bottom of this valley of grief. Maybe I have. Despite losing you, there still remain those I love. I'm still in sorrow, but I refuse to succumb to it. Progress is slow but aided by small steps. Every day I make a list of things to do. Some are routine, like maintaining some aspect of the household or myself. Others are more external or growth oriented like working on this book, answering a letter from a friend, or sorting through a box pulled from storage.

Full Stop

L: A mix of emotions rattle me as September arrives. The 18th marks the anniversary of your death, and the 29th your birthday. How can it be a year already? I'm not ready to allow it; to acknowledge it. But time pays no heed to sorrow, or mourning, or pain. It just advances; whether I'm aligned or not, doesn't matter. Time marks its path through the void bringing September with it.

After a year without you, I sometimes get a little tired of my periods of lethargy. All I seem to do is simple chores and read. I have to remind myself I'm still grieving and allow myself time to rebalance. I have to remind myself to stop judging myself, I'm not okay yet.

I don't want to memorialize the 18th, but the date is drilled into my brain. So, I relive your final weeks against my will. I am alone again, as every day I have been; but the milestone intensifies the solitude and my isolation. I would just as soon ignore this hurtle and focus on your birthday. At least there it seems as if there may be more opportunity to celebrate your life, rather than mark your death.

My natural inclination is to withdraw on your birthday, but Whitney has reached out. I think her natural inclination is like yours—to offer comfort and support on this difficult day. To be together and share our love for you. She made your recipe for vegetable stew with dumplings in your honor, and our tight little family unit ate heartily and remembered the magic you brought to our lives.

The Doorknob

L: Every day of your cancer journey was filled with emotion, fear, and sorrow. Early on there were moments of hope as well, but the more we learned, the more hope shrank. There were too many low points, and the day you died was the worst. Whatever resilience I had must be part of the human condition, because initially I had no desire to recover. Yet, in the months that have accrued I have progressed.

For me, grief follows the path of two steps forward, one step back. Every time a warm feeling of progress rises up, I'm soon reminded the journey isn't over, the path to healing is a crooked, rutted road. Greif is not linear.

As Harry was leaving for work this morning, he told me the doorknob on the door between the house and the garage was stuck. I sighed to myself. Another problem, another thing to be dealt with.

It was stuck fast. The handle wouldn't budge, not even a wiggle. I tried it from the other side with no difference. Something internal was hosed. Fortunately, Parkrose Hardware opens at 7am, so I got a replacement well before the place was packed with customers. Yes, I still try to shop when stores are sparse, a habit sprung during Covid, that remains.

I learned how to slip a lock when I was a doorman at the theater where we met. The doorman's room was a sort of locker room where you changed from your street clothes into your doorman outfit. I guess there was a key, but most of the time everyone just slipped the lock with a library card or some other hunk of plastic, because it was faster. You can't slip every lock with this trick, but when you have to it often works well.

Anyway, I got the door open, removed the old knob, and installed the new one.

If you were here, I still would have dealt with this myself. But with you gone, it came with an ache of loneliness. There was no witness. Another reminder I am alone, without your presence—even if in another room in the house somewhere. I didn't understand that knowing you were there made these sorts of things better, easier; until now. You were the insider, the intimate witness of my life; as I was yours.

I think this idea of witnessing our lives is a contributing factor to the rise of social media. We all want someone to care about what happens to us or what we do. We need it.

When these minor setbacks occur, I try to remember that if I can survive losing you, I can survive just about anything. Sometimes it only requires time and attention. Other times it involves getting help from outside—friends or vendors with the expertise to solve a particular problem. Sometimes it helps to set aside the problem for a day or two (if that's possible) and allow my subconscious to develop a plan for how to tackle it. The mind is an amazing thing.

Walking in the Rain

L: Portland is famous for its rain. Just across the river, in Vancouver, Washington it's the same. I've cried in grief more than once while behind the wheel in the rain at night. I'll never forget driving through the heart of the city from Good Sam to OHSU up on the hill in November 1988. Dark, rainy, with only a general idea of where I was going. Leaving you in maternity in one hospital to be with our son who had been taken by ambulance to the ICU in another, where they had the best facilities to try and save him.

Decades later it was October, a year and a month after you died. I'm no poet, but the rain and sadness bubbled up with this:

Another dreary October morning.

Ain't got no 'brella.

Ain't got no cap.

But you won't see me crying.

That's why I'm walking in the rain.

Your rapid decline was a waking nightmare, a living Hell. As grief took hold after your death, I wondered when this nightmare would end. I guess it doesn't. What changes is the sting; the mark it leaves. I'm not sure we heal exactly, but English doesn't seem to have a better word, so we use heal.

The pain and sorrow become less intense as the months accrue. Denial gives way to acceptance because at some point your absence is undeniable.

Hospice nurses tell us that death ends the suffering of their patients. As the body begins to shut down, the patient's mind can calm and let go. Maybe there is a complementary path for the bereaved. The death of sorrow is slow and painful, but it's comforting to think there will come a peaceful day when one can finally let go of most of the grief.

In therapy, I was told there is no way around it, I must go through the valley of grief. My grief does not define who I am, it is what I am experiencing. However slowly, I must keep moving through the valley. Patience is a challenge. I don't always want to face this sorrow. The road zig zags with obstacles and setbacks, but I must have faith that the path I'm on will eventually lead out of the valley. I long for a day, some future day, when my grief has been replaced with only thoughts of my love for you.

Time is no comfort. As the months pass, it's easy to feel reconciling grief is taking too long. I'll never get beyond it. I can only put my faith in the process and in patience. Aim to move forward. There is no other way.

I loved nestling here in our home with you. Our

home still brings me comfort even in your absence, because part of you remains. I continue to find warmth and love here, so I will care for it and continue to shape it in your memory, in this afterlife.

After several months the electric candle I put in our bedroom window failed, so I threw it out. But I found that I missed it, so I got another. I don't feel you here in our bedroom with me at night, but if you ever stop by, it's a sign I'm still thinking about you so much of the time.

After many months of mourning, I have finally found the resolve to return to writing. I feel very motivated to write this book. It's therapy for my sorrow. It honors your memory, and I hope it will be useful to others who find themselves in this same lonely place.

I wonder if I'll continue to write, when this book is finished. Will I return to fiction, publishing, or look for other outlets for my creative self? I'd like to think I'll return to fiction, but only time will tell.

Reaching out to socialize is still hard for me. It always was, but now more than ever, without you as my safe harbor, my touchstone. Everything I've learned about grief stresses the importance of connections in moving forward and staying positive. I'm doing okay with our family and friends, but I have not made any new friends since you died. I'll get there, because I know at some point I'll need to pave a new path.

Finitude

L: We're not immortal but act as if we are. Mortality has new weight since you died. It seems ridiculous to say this, but in the before times, it was almost as if it didn't apply to us. It was something that happened to other people. Not today. Now it's top of mind, a daily shadow that colors my perspective and decisions.

I think it was Louise who turned me onto Jane Friedman's *Electric Speed* newsletter. Friedman mentioned a book by Oliver Burkeman, *Four Thousand Weeks* aka *Time Management for Mortals*. It's basically a book about the brevity of life with advice on how to focus on what's most important to spend your limited time here on.

What's the opposite of infinity? Finitude. Since I don't have forever, it's high time to focus on importance over everything else. Burkeman's "Ten Tools for Embracing Your Finitude" are worth the price of the volume, but the whole thing is, as *The Wall Street Journal* said: "Well worth your extremely limited time."

I'm no master of Burkeman's ten tools, but they're worth revisiting on a regular basis to help make the most of what's left. And what are those things? For me, the basics are devoting a reasonable amount of time to maintaining health and home, enriching relationships with family and friends, and downsizing my possessions so Harry and Whitney will have less to deal with when I'm gone. While I am open to devoting more energy to health, I'm also constantly looking for ways to streamline home maintenance and purging possessions. A few years ago, I would have organized a garage sale; now I'm more likely to make donations, and if I can find a place that picks things up, so much the better.

What about joy? Without you, the greatest joy of my life is gone. What remains may be diminished, but the things I liked doing in the before times, still make me happy. I ponder the things that have brought me joy in the past to help me function in this new life. At their most basic these are creativity, clarity, recognition, and love. For me, creativity can be passive like reading or watching TV. It's also making things, like writing this book. Clarity is the search for understanding, which can mean the big questions, but also many little ones. Clarity encompasses things like organizing, anything that helps put order into my world. I can use this need to help drive the many downsizing tasks that still need to be done. Recognition is mostly a desire for external approval. I wish it weren't so but try as I may to find satisfaction internally, I still crave validation from outside. It's a weakness. Love drives me toward family and friends and perhaps at times to challenge my comfort zone.

Over the Rainbow

L: This morning, I was listening to a presentation, published as an audiobook; *Embracing the Unknown* by Pema Chödrön. She talks about the impermanence of life, and, in fact, the impermanence of everything. My happiest moments and even my greatest sorrows are transient. When joy comes, embrace it and celebrate it for the gift it is. When sorrow arrives, no matter how deep, know that it too is transient. Try to believe a better time will come.

If I can begin to embrace the impermanence of life's little moments, it can begin to change my overall perspective. Everything is transient, so enjoy the good and try not to sweat the bad so much.

As a child, the first time I heard Judy Garland sing "Over the Rainbow" in *The Wizard of Oz*, I was overwhelmed. The song was so beautiful, yet it made me sad. It painted a picture of a perfect place, somewhere I felt incapable of ever reaching. How could I ever get there?

One of my favorite gag cartoons shows a man talking to a travel agent. His destination? "Someplace where troubles melt like lemon drops." Ain't that the truth? I'd love to be transported to this vision of perfection and get to stay there forever. Like a vision of the hereafter.

When I was a kid, I thought "Over the Rainbow" made me sad because I could never in my whole life imagine creating anything as beautiful or wonderful as that song. I was at a loss.

So many decades later, I think my emotions were closer to grief. "Over the Rainbow" in my mind was perfect. I was grieving the impermanence of that moment of perfection when I first heard Garland, because it couldn't last. Many years later, I felt similar emotions when I watched the Beatles on that rooftop in London singing "Across the Universe."

I would've thought the concept of impermanence would be obvious after your death. But I was too stricken by sorrow, too stunned by reality, to imagine anything in a larger context. We search all our lives for understanding and meaning. Sometimes it takes someone outside ourselves to put the things we're feeling into words. Now that time has elapsed, I can listen again. Impermanence resonates the more it sinks in.

When the car insurance renewal was coming up, I sold the SmartCar. If/when something eventually goes wrong with the VW, I may regret not having a backup, but I figure a rental, or a few rideshares will be less expensive than owning a car that sits idle. I loved both the Mini Cooper and the Smart-Car, but cars are impermanent, and I'm happy to have two less possessions to maintain.

It's only been 14 months since you died. All this time. All my grief work. At this moment, none of it matters. I still miss you so much. I miss being in love with you and holding you in my arms. It feels like I should be farther along. I think I'm doing okay, but then I have a bad night, or I suddenly feel as bad as I did months ago. It makes it hard to feel like I'm making progress. I know from doing difficult things like quitting smoking, that setbacks are part of the process, not failures. Maybe the same is true for grief, but grief is a different kind of challenge, and this grief is harder than any I've ever faced. I can only put my faith in the process. Be kind and gentle with myself—even now after 14 months.

Sometimes I can find a little project that engages me, so I dive in, and it holds my attention for a little while. But when it's done, I'm back on my own again, lonely and longing for your love.

I'm still struggling to find my way.

Standards

L: I'll never forget the argument about housekeeping at the house on Jennifer Street where you lived with seven roommates during college. The women were annoyed about the men not keeping up their end of the shared housekeeping. The conversation I heard was between a couple, where he maintained that the men did contribute. The conflict arose because the men and women had different standards of what was acceptable. I was a guest at the time, so I stayed out of it. When I moved in with you to become the eighth roommate, I took my turn making dinner and washing dishes. I don't recall further conflict about housekeeping.

One of the sidebars of losing you that wasn't immediately apparent as I floundered in grief and the reality of being alone, are things like housekeeping. As we grew older together we migrated towards the more traditional gender roles modeled by our parents; where you did most of the indoor tasks and I did most of outdoor stuff. I still did vacuuming, and nearly always washed the dishes or loaded the dishwasher, but we generally did the tasks we were most adept at, rooted in our upbringing.

Now, the housekeeping baton has passed to me. The standards you set are a stretch for me. Part of it I suspect goes back to our old roommate's perspective, or rather, what was behind his perspective. I just don't notice the same things you did. My vision expands when I'm expecting company or even noticing how dusty a certain corner is after the guests have arrived.

Another factor—now that you're gone—is that my task list has doubled. I don't want to spend twice as much time making everything nicey nice. Your death evokes how precious a gift my remaining time is, so although I would like to honor your standards, I must face reality. My standards are lower, perhaps inferior; my goal is to streamline as much as possible.

A few things like window washing and dusting are especially hard for me. I hardly notice when they're needed. I failed window washing 101. They end up streaked instead of dirty. I'm just going to ignore them until it bothers me.

I must change my mindset and remind myself

that a few whispers of dust are okay. I have more important things to attend to like health, relationships, and creativity. I want to train myself to celebrate a little mess as a sign of time spent wisely (elsewhere) rather than hound myself over tasks with a short shelf life.

A friend advises me to hire a professional once or twice a year to give the place a good going over. If we could change places, I'd encourage you to do this in a heartbeat.

Growing up—through Mom's example, I was taught the cleaning regimen was a routine—as in once a week. Do everything whether it needs it or not. For most of my life this was my playbook. Your approach was more spontaneous. When you notice something, take care of it. Now that I'm alone, I'm adopting your approach. It honors your spirit, and it's more practical for this new life in which most everything falls to me.

One other observation: The numerous unassigned tasks, like loading the dishwasher, vacuuming, or clearing countertops were easy to let slide when there was a chance you might handle it. Whenever I had something more important to do, I felt less attached to a maintenance task. If I noticed something was still undone a few hours later, then

I'd address it myself. With you gone, I know that whatever needs doing is my task. It does take more time and effort, but the "who's going to do it" wild-card is gone. Why couldn't I have had this attitude all along? If it needs doing, I own it.

There are many roles in life. Without you, I'm no longer husband/spouse. A major part of my identity is gone. I feel part of my value in this life has disappeared. Beyond learning to live with my grief, I must also begin to redefine myself outside the role of husband. I still am father and friend, but even those roles are affected by your death. In the before times, I didn't give much thought to roles. I just went about my day, doing things that needed doing. In a way, that's the feeling I might aim for in this afterlife.

Before, I had at least a half dozen roles that were separate from you, our kids, or our friends. And I had a group of separate friends as well. Which of them still engage me now, and why? The answers may offer some clues as to how my afterlife will evolve.

Poetry

L: It's been a while, and I sometimes think I should be leaving the valley of grief. I would like to be motivated to get on with my life. But something always happens. I had dinner with friends and your absence at our table was so obvious, it reminded me my partner now is loneliness. I had a couple glasses of wine with dinner and drank a shot of vodka when I got home. Why? Just sadness over the reality of being without you.

Today is Dec 10, 2024. I have lived one day longer than you, my sweet love.

How do I know this? Because I can't stop thinking about you and your absence. Pangs of survivor's guilt have resurfaced. Pangs of guilt I have not felt for a while.

After dinner, I took my vodka and got in bed and played with my phone. I cocooned. It feels like I shouldn't have to cocoon so much anymore, but the reality is I still need to escape the world. It's getting so I wish I could get through this, but I can't. Patience. I just have to accept how I feel and act accordingly.

At some point or other, David Kessler advised, "This isn't about self-help. It's about self-acceptance."

Some days it feels as if I have made progress. But I must face the fact that I'm not "over" this yet.

My familiarity with poetry was (and remains) limited, but Emily Hockaday sent me several of her poems once, giving me a peek into the poet's world. In 2022, Cornerstone Press published a collection of her poems, *Naming the Ghost*, with reflections on the birth of her daughter and the death of her father. She combines insights on life's two greatest milestones: birth and death; with love, sorrow, honesty, and comfort.

In 2023, one of our couple friends gave me a copy of Gregory Orr's *Poetry as Survival*. There are poems included in the volume, but it's more a book *about* poetry than *of* poetry. Orr details the tragic loss of his brother in his childhood, his struggle to come to terms with the loss, and the solace he found in poetry. In the final section he explains the poetry of renowned poets like William Wordsworth, Keats, Walt Whitman, Emily Dickinson, Wilfred Owen, Sylvia Plath, Stanley Kunitz, and Theodore Roethke.

In 2024, Louise and Kent gave me a copy of Billy Collins' *Water, Water*. A few months later, I saw it in the library's collection of audio books and checked it out. I wasn't sure how poetry would work in this format; listening to one poem after another without a pause to reflect between them. But I figured it was worth a try. I'm very glad I did, because Collins is the narrator, and who better to read poems than the poet himself. His style, subjects, and voice clicked with me immediately.

He writes about life's mundane moments. His observations are clever, poignant, and edifying. We're always getting advice to live in the moment, but most moments are mundane. Collins is able to examine these precious, unmomentous moments, and express their importance—the importance of now—in a way I've never experienced before. There are individual poems that stand out, but the collection has a power of its own.

Suddenly, I realize I'm forgetting the poetry I've always loved best: lyrics. I don't automatically think of lyrics as poetry, but of course they are. Poetry wrapped in a memorable tune that draws you back again and again. You and I grew up with the British Invasion, and I still love the big-name bands of that era. Later, I was drawn to the singer/songwriters of the 70s and 80s. Their lyrics went beyond boy/girl romance and explored deeper feelings and life in general. This has always been my main source of poetry, and I turn toward it more than ever now.

Stuff

L: I feel compelled to deal with all of our stuff.

Mostly, I want to unburden Harry and Whitney with all the stuff I should have dealt with following your death. I know you feel/felt the same. In fact, you were far less attached to possessions than I am. There will be enough of my stuff for H&W to deal with when I go, so I'd like to have the rest of it sorted before that.

I had thought of documenting everything with a photo and a description of its meaning. Perhaps not a bad notion, but as time goes on it seems more and more daunting. Plus, when I think about "who cares?" it's hard to justify. The majority of this stuff means the most to me. It's hard to imagine H&W reading through pages of memories once, let alone more than that. The notion is nice, but I think the reality would be just like photo albums and boxes full of artifacts that were never unpacked after the last move, now seven years in the rearview. For these reasons, I've decided not to pursue photographing the stuff or documenting it. Even things like the Irving Biehn painting. An original, the artist gave to my parents as a wedding gift lo these many years ago. It still means a lot to me, but its sentimental value diminishes over time and generations. It's a nice painting, but certainly not everyone's cup of tea either.

I just have to accept that many things will be lost to time, just as they have always been for past generations. I can't imagine our granddaughter being delighted to display the original Biehn in her home long after I'm gone, and grateful to know where it came from.

I may regret taking action to rid myself of things, but I feel a strange compulsion to do it. These things hold their value as reminders or tributes to the past. But they are impermanent, ephemeral. The memories they make are inside me, in my heart, not in the objects themselves. I've categorized them to help me sort out their fate:

My Mementos

There are items like the Christmas music box, that are sentimental to me. It's in less than perfect condition and has spent 95% of the past decades in storage. It has been brought out a few times for Christmas, but I don't think you were particularly fond of it, so it wasn't always on display. These are the types of things I'll have to decide whether to keep, donate, or trash.

Our Mementos

There are things we bought together, like the Thomas McKnight silkscreen print. These things are on a sliding scale as to their level of meaning.

With you gone, their meaning to me has increased, just because they remind me of our lives together. Only those things that I'm not personally fond of would I consider parting with.

Your Mementos

These fall into two categories: Those I like personally, and those I don't. Some I want simply because I know they were sentimental to you and that makes them feel more valuable to me. Others, I'm less certain about the depth of your connection, so if I don't like their aesthetics myself, it's probably best to downsize.

Your Display Items

You had drawers full of things like candles. I want to pare these down to what fits my afterlife. You were big into holiday decorations. I enjoyed being around your displays, benefiting from your arrangements and efforts, but I have minimal desire to try and mimic your passion in this arena. These are more boxes I need to pare down or eliminate.

Artwork

This is a tough one. I'm still torn about capturing artwork and documenting it—both yours and mine. It would be a lot of work, but I'm still not ready to purge this stuff. It could be just as useless as mementos, but for now I can't let go of it.

Your Family's Items

These are things like silverware or silver-plated items and furniture. Mostly, they meant more to you than to me. I do like the aesthetics of some of the pieces of furniture, but others are kind of clunky. For example, I love the aesthetics of your grandmother's desk, but it's uncomfortable to sit at, heavy, and its storage compartments are nearly useful. So, what to do?

I think the drop-leaf table was used in the kitchen of your parent's house. You probably grew up eating most of your meals at it, and maybe even doing your homework on it. It had a lot of sentimental value for you. But it's also a bit unwieldy, heavy, and its leaves bang every time I move it to vacuum. If not for your attachments, it would be easy for me to part with it. So, I'm still processing this one.

As I purge stuff, I feel like I'm erasing parts of your past, our past, and even parts of mine. This makes me just want to ignore it all and leave it lay; just focus on other things. Trouble is, I see this stuff all the time, and it needles me to find closure. And I don't want to leave it all for H&W to deal with. They'll have their hands full with what's left.

I was talking to Whitney about some of this, and

she passed on some good ideas. As I go through things, pick the stuff that's easiest to part with first. Set aside anything that gives me pause. Maybe I'll do a little unconscious processing in the meantime and when I come back to it, a decision may come more easily. Another thought: if there are several trays (and there are), pick out the best and get rid of the rest.

Going through your clothing was both easy and difficult. Since I can't use most of them, that was the easy part. Things you wore often, and your favorites were more difficult. Fortunately, Whitney led the purge of your closet. She took some things for herself. She took a pile of others that she plans to cut into squares for a quilt or throw that would transform your clothes into something to honor your memory and still be useful. The third pile was things I felt comfortable donating, and there were plenty.

A few things, like your favorite T-shirts I added to my closet. And I was happy to discover I could wear many of your old pajamas, so I kept them all. I love sleeping in them and being reminded of you at night.

As I sort through your possessions I try to honor you but also face the fact that you're no longer here and will never use them again. "If it's worth keeping, it should be used." That means taking art and decor items out of storage—either use them or dispose of them. Another idea I've found helpful is forgiveness. Sometimes I make the wrong decision. I can accept that. It's better to move forward than be perfect. Sorting through everything is a lot of work, so I take it slow.

Margareta Magnusson's *The Swedish Art of Death Cleaning* is on my list of books to read, but I'm already framing my purging in that context. Someday, should I live long enough, I may want to downsize to a condo without a yard. This will be far, far better for Harry when I'm gone, and for me it'll be far less work to maintain. Having this goal brings clarity to purging. If it won't fit in a smaller place, I can't justify holding onto it. When the day comes to move, whatever possessions I take along must fit.

I'll know I'm ready when all the extra spaces in this house are empty.

Where is God?

L: I never asked you directly if you believed in God. I'm pretty sure your parents were believers, so I imagine it was part of your childhood, but I gather not a dominating part. I know what you thought about morality and kindness, because you acted accordingly. Perhaps not God, but I know you thought about the power of the Universe. And what else?

This "missing think" is also part of my loss and our family's. You held so much history—your own, your parents' and grandparents', our childrens', and more. It's sad to know that we can't ask you about so many things now.

I was brought up Lutheran, and my family attended church every Sunday during the catechism years of both my sister and I—so roughly five or six years between the two of us. In hindsight, I think this was the desire of my mom; my dad just went along. Afterward, I was never particularly religious, but I have leaned on God in times of trouble. As John Lennon succinctly expressed, "God is a concept by which we measure our pain."

My faith has waned as I've aged, but it crashed with your diagnosis and losing battle with cancer. You were an angel as far as I'm concerned. How could any God allow such a beautiful person to die the way you did? I felt that if I ever prayed again, it would be to your spirit, not to God. Even the faith of one as famously devout as C.S. Lewis was shaken by his wife's death. "You never know how much you really believe anything until its truth or falsehood becomes a matter of life and death to you," he wrote in *A Grief Observed*.

I have mellowed a bit in the months following. I'm less certain about outright abandoning God. But I also feel less certain about embracing Him. After Colin died I read *When Bad Things Happen to Good People*. It was very helpful during that time, but that was so long ago, its message had slipped away. I only remembered, it helped at that time. So, I read it again. Kushner faced a crisis of faith when his son succumbed to a rare disease that rapidly aged him. He felt the same emotions, questions, and doubts I had. He explored every angle and finally redefined God, not as a judgmental, vengeful, all-powerful being, but as a compassionate, forgiving, loving being, who cannot change fate. The solace He provides is entirely love. Knowing He loves everyone no matter what, can help give one the strength to face life's hardships and nightmares. This concept of God is far more appealing than any other I've heard.

I'm still a skeptic, but in the absence of proof, I think skepticism is the only rational choice. If God is real and God is love, then when I pray to your spirit, to your Love in His place, He'll understand.

The bereaved look for signs their loved ones are still with them. Sometimes they appear in dreams or perhaps in events that seem to be more than mere coincidence. C.S. Lewis wrote: "You don't have a soul. You are a soul. You have a body."

In counterpoint, I think it's true that we tend to find what we're looking for. Especially, when we never stop looking.

I wrote earlier about expectations, and your advice about its pitfalls. The same can be said for assumptions. I assume the old will die and the young will live. But what happens when a child dies before his parent? The hard truth is that assumptions are half-truths at best. Better to cherish today than assume a promise of tomorrow. Life is unfair, or rather, fairness applies only where rules exist.

Your death came out of the blue; sudden and unexpected. It's easy to label it as unfair, but it was neither fair nor unfair. It just happened. No one is to blame. It's just hard to accept because it's so difficult to bear.

I've been confronted by the lack of medical salvation more often than not in my life. I've learned the promise of medicine often belies its reality. Medicine is important, sometimes it's miraculous, but it is still in its infancy. To believe otherwise is not reality.

It's not true, but it feels logical that people older than you should have gone before you. You were such an inspiration, and you took great care of yourself most of your life. And yet here we are. This is not justice—or a mistaken ideal of justice. This is reality. Some people die and some people live. None of us gets to choose. Fate is fickle and unpredictable. All we can do is the best we can and greet every day as another gift we may not receive again.

On what would have been our 50th anniversary, I did nothing to celebrate. I'm grateful for our 48 years of marriage, but I mostly felt sad and numb that day. More cocooning, solitude, looking at my phone. That night I reminisced to Harry about the six months you and I lived in Racine, where we were married.

Facing Life Alone

L: You told me that you had cataracts a while back, and even though your eye doctor told you they weren't bad yet, the glare of the oncoming headlights when driving at night was a problem. I'm grateful you never had to go through a hip replacement or cataract surgery. I'll take solace where

I can find it...

Turns out I had cataracts too. My doctor told me that everyone gets them eventually, if you live long enough. The average age for the operation is 75. I was aiming for that, but one day I developed another problem. This was kind of like a floater, but instead of a black spec it was more like a fuzzy blob that floats around in my left eye, my good one.

I knew the cataract surgery wouldn't fix that, but I figured any improvement would be a good thing, so I went for an evaluation. Yep, I was eligible. It was a bigger deal in my mind than it turned out to be, but I didn't look forward to it. This was the first big medical event I had to face alone.

You can choose what kind of replacement lens you want. Do you want to be farsighted or nearsighted? I think a few people even do one of each. I couldn't imagine that, but I guess your brain sorts things out in short order. I've been nearsighted since grade school, but I choose farsighted so I wouldn't need glasses to drive. That was particularly helpful during the period between the first surgery and the end of the recovery period of the second, because I could drive during almost that entire month. That would not have been the case if I'd opted for nearsightedness.

The first hurtle was logistics. You're not allowed to drive home after the surgery, and as it turns out, my guy wants to see you later the same day to ensure the healing is on track. I first turned to Whitney and Sean, but the baby was due right around the same time, and they didn't feel comfortable committing to my schedule, when theirs was in flux.

I thought about asking friends, but they all live in Portland, and it would be kind of a big ask for them to drive 20 miles to get here and then spend most of their day shepherding me to and fro for my appointments. So, I asked Harry to manage the rideshare app for me throughout the day. He was glad to help.

The nurse at the clinic gave me the highlights of what to expect. I called up some friends and spoke to one who'd recently had it done. Hearing about her experience helped lessen my anxiety.

I made sure to thoroughly stock the larder before the surgery, not knowing how long it would be before I could drive. Besides, a full refrigerator is always a comfort.

I was a little nervous about going. I sorely missed your presence and moral support. I knew there was an eye drops regimen afterward and knew you couldn't play nurse mate. Oh well, this was only the first time I'd have to face something medical without you. Better something as routine and safe as this than something more dire.

The operation was done at a hospital, rather than the clinic. I was prepped in a hospital bed with an IV and monitors while waiting my turn. No food since dinner the day before. The doc stopped by beforehand to answer any final questions. Everybody double- and triple-checked which eye was being done. They even marked it with a black dot above my eyebrow. Not such a big deal thing for number one, but absolutely critical for number two!

There were two analgesics. Eye drops to numb the eye, and a mild general to calm even the most anxious patient. The operation itself only lasts a few minutes. I felt no pain whatsoever during the procedure. I imagined my head and eyeball would somehow be clamped in place, and I'd have to keep my eye stationery. But it wasn't that dramatic. The doctor had the hard part, but he was very experienced, and everything went smoothly. There is some risk, but it's low. Cataract surgery is the most common surgery of all, ranking above C-section, joint replacement, and circumcision.

There was no gauze or eye patch covering the surgery afterward. They kept me in recovery for a half hour or so and then said I could go. Harry engaged a rideshare and took me home.

The eye drop regimen begins right away. There are two medications, Prednisolone (pink cap) and Prolensa (grey cap). Pink is to reduce inflammation; grey is to prevent infection. You can take OTC pain relievers if needed, but I didn't. Your absence was salient. The first week of eye drops is four times a day, second three times, third twice, and fourth once. Each round requires the two different drops, with five to ten minutes between. I got tired of doing it after a few days but stayed on schedule anyway. Although the bottles are small, there was more than enough drops. Important, because I missed the target at least several times a day but still never ran out. I should note, the prescriptions were issued so they could be filled prior to the surgery, so I didn't need to drive with fuzzy eyesight. For some reason the insurance balked at the Rx for the second eye, and the pharmacy had to do a workaround, so I'd have them pre-op for the second operation.

Four hours after the surgery I took a rideshare to the clinic. The check-in was short, and the doc declared everything A-okay. The clinic is just over a mile from our house, so I opted to walk home rather than rack up another fare. It was super sunny, so I wore the wraparound sunglasses the clinic had issued prior to the surgery. The vision in my left eye was quite blurry, so I relied on my right to navigate the sidewalk home. You're advised to take it easy for 24 hours, but I didn't figure walking was too strenuous. I made it okay with no detriments.

I didn't do much the rest of the day. I couldn't read or watch TV very well, so I think I mostly listened to music, snacked, and fiddled with eye drops. It's okay to shower a few hours after the operation, just keep your face dry and do not allow any shower spray to strike your eyelids. Since I'd showered that morning, I left that milestone for the next day.

Along with sunglasses, the clinic also issued an eye guard. This is a clear plastic patch that fits over your eye, resting outside your eye socket, and taped into place. I had to look for a video online to see how to attach it. You're supposed to put it on at night, so you don't inadvertently put any pressure whatsoever on your eye while you're asleep. I wore it for about five sleeps and then quit. It's a little annoying, but bearable.

The first morning the eyesight of my left eye was very blurry. There was no pain as such, but it felt "scratchy," a feeling that was helped intermittently by rounds of eye drops. This scratchiness lasted on and off for about a week, until it faded away entirely. By the afternoon of the first full day, the blurriness was clearing, and I was able to read a little. By the next morning, my eyesight was clear and sharp. I went out for a coffee to see how a short drive would feel. It was fine, and the by the afternoon I felt comfortable driving across the river to pick-up Harry from work.

In the following days, things felt better and better. I was still wearing my glasses for the correction for my right eye, but of course the lens over the left was no longer helping. I ended up carefully removing the left lens and that was better. Things were still a little wonky during this interim period and I was starting to look forward to getting on with the next operation.

Harry and I repeated the pattern for the right eye, two weeks after the left. The doc advised that patients often feel a little more awake during the second procedure. For me, it seemed about the same. Everything went smoothly again until I got to recovery. This time, when the nurses asked me how I was doing, I said, "Fine, just a little dizzy. No, not dizzy, I feel a little faint." My blood pressure and oxygenation were normal, but my heart rate was in the 40s. Weird. As we got to talking, it came out that I hadn't eaten anything since about 3:00 pm the previous day. The anesthesiologist brought me a turkey sandwich and an orange juice. An hour later I was skirting the 60s, so they released me.

By now it was late enough that we could go directly from the hospital to the clinic, bypassing a wait at home, and save the extra rideshares. Everything checked out and we rode home afterward.

The second recovery went even better than the first, and I could see quite well after the first night's sleep. Now I could discard my old glasses entirely. I used reading glasses to see things closer than about a foot, foot-and-a-half.

The doctor called to check-in the day after the surgery, both times. Two weeks later, I went back to the clinic. My eyes had healed well. Most of the inflammation was gone, so he tested my vision and wrote a prescription for progressive lenses. I ordered glasses online and got them a few weeks later.

I was grateful for Harry's help through this experience, but I sorely missed your love and support. And I surely missed your help with what felt like a never-ending routine of eye drops. Nonetheless, I made it through. I wore one of your old t-shirts at each of the operations, for luck, and to feel you near. It wasn't a bad experience, but I'm also grateful you never had to go through it yourself.

Of course, I don't know the future. But I can't help wondering about it. What if I had the surgery and learned three months later, I'd developed some untreatable disease? As I age, this is my new reality, one that losing you helped me understand. I can't stop living over what might happen tomorrow, but the more I grasp my own mortality, the better I can appreciate today.

Months Seventeen to Twenty-Four
Get Over It

L: The biggest epiphany I gained from David Kessler's *Finding Meaning: The Sixth Stage of Grief Workbook* was reflecting on the ways my father modeled grief when I was a teen. When my mom was hospitalized with cancer and it was certain she would die, my dad called me into the living room and gave me the bad news. He started to break up and excused himself, retreating to my parents' bedroom. That was the only time in my life I had ever seen him cry. I was left in the living room, stunned and unable to move. When he returned a few minutes later, he apologized for breaking up. That was the only time in my life I ever heard him apologize.

My mom went on to have chemo and radiation treatments that bought her about another year of life. When her cancer returned she was again hospitalized and died in the middle of the night alone. The hospital called my dad, and he woke me up to tell me.

He had her cremated, which was her wish. I never saw the ashes and never knew what happened to them. There was no ceremony and no further discussion. Her absence from our lives was acknowledged, but my dad never mentioned his sorrow or grief, although I know that he loved her.

I don't blame him for any of this. I don't know how grief was modeled for him as he grew up, but I imagine it was similar. Don't cry and don't dwell on the loss. I know he had a sister that died in a fire when he was a child, so he'd experienced a tragedy early in his life. In hindsight, I wish I'd asked a lot more questions about all these things, but he was a product of his era. Men don't talk about feelings— maybe even, men don't have feelings. If you do, get over it.

I'm Still Here

L: At some point, the throes of grief will subside enough for me to fully grasp that I'm still here. (It's tempting to preface this with "like it or not," because without you is so much less than with you.) But life. for the living, goes on. I don't have a death wish. I'm grateful to still be here, but I'm still lost trying to figure out what this means.

Since my group therapy doesn't address this head-on, I started searching for some books that might shed some light on this. *Learning to Live Alone* by Bob Hurmence offered some hints. This is a self-published book, written by a guy who was about 80 when it came out in 2007. What I most appreciated about his book was his candor and willingness to share his experiences of losing his wife. Theirs was a long marriage, and the story of his wife's demise and its impact on him was moving and resonant. Hearing from someone who's lost a spouse is more powerful than just about anything else for the recently widowed.

Besides the emotional loss, there's also the practical loss of the person who made a major contribution to your household and the logistics of your lives together. The most useful part of the book's second half was Hurmence's acknowledgement of the impact on his afterlife, on everything he had to learn, and all the considerations that confronted him.

I'm not able to tackle all my goals every day. But keeping a list is helpful and it's a good reminder of what's most important. I do some housekeeping or yardwork most days, and I'm always thinking about ways to do chores more efficiently, so I have more time for more important things like connection and growth.

The other book in this vein that's worth mentioning is Barbara Feldon's *Living Alone and Loving It*. I had fond memories of Feldon from *Get Smart*, so I gave it a try. Part of it is autobiographical, but she has lived alone for quite some time and offers advice about it. Like Feldon, there is a growing number of women who live alone and like it that way. Still, relationships are the key to a healthy mental state, and Feldon provides tips on how to foster them. I have more work to do in this area. Progress, pushing against comfort zones, is hard work.

Other Couples

L: Growing up, like you, I learned to be a people-pleaser. My behavior was often guided with an eye toward never deliberately doing something to displease Mom or Dad. This may be part of why I lean toward external approval.

The idea of unconditional love is overused. When I think of God, surely His love is unconditional. Your love felt unconditional. But many times in my life, the love or like I've felt from others has been conditional. If it's true for others, perhaps it's a contributing factor in the rise of divorce during our lives. Time changes people, and their love can't always adapt to the changes—it was conditional.

I think grief is not a welcome topic in many circles. How much does my concern to people-please affect my grief? When I feel tears welling up at the grocery store, do I let them flow, or try to get a grip? It's better to feel the feelings, but my concerns over other's impressions are tough to overcome. Although so much of my day involves thinking about your absence, I'm very unlikely to bring it up to strangers, acquaintances, or even sometimes friends or family. I don't want to be a downer, make others feel uncomfortable, or remind them of their own grief.

When it dominates my moments, it might be better to share those feelings and just be authentic.

There is something very special about getting together with other couples, especially those made up of people you both truly enjoy being with. During all the years we've known our besties I don't recall thinking much about if our primary connection was you or me. There were no thoughts of favorites or feelings of anxiety. But the dynamics change when you're alone.

I wonder if my next visit with couple friends will be not just different, but less enthusiastic. The balance of our coupledom is gone. Will our friends feel uncomfortable visiting with just me? Will they feel about me as they used to about us? Will your absence tip the scales so much so that they'd rather not get together as often or shift toward larger events that include more people than just me? Do they see their future when they look at me now? Even the author C.S. Lewis pondered these questions in his memoirs.

There's comfort in being part of a couple in social situations. Particularly, something like a party. Not things I've given much thought to in the past several decades. Not when I had you, my infallible, emotional anchor for support.

Well, that's not the way it is anymore. Since you died, I have joined our besties to celebrate birthdays or some other milestone, and I'm happy my concerns were unfounded. Our couple friends were equally welcoming to me, as they'd been when you were here. I'm grateful. And your absence is acknowledged and honored, not denied or ignored. Life moves forward, and it seems our friendships do as well.

I've only been to one party in the past 18 months.

Fortunately, I knew everyone there, so I was able to function well. I do wonder how I'd fare if I attended some future event where I knew only a few of the guests. A therapist would advise me to challenge my introversion, but I'm not sure I'm up for that yet. I guess time will settle the question.

These changes in relationships—we to me—are one category of what's different now. Change was constant before you died. Now it is part of everything that touches my life. I still feel tinges of guilt/sorrow over the changes I make sometimes, or the dynamic changes created by your absence. I try to temper these emotions by honoring your memory. As long as I live, I will continue to move forward through time. It's okay to live in the present and to make my own changes. Sometimes I just need to remind myself that my changes are not disloyalty to you. They are part of the reality of my afterlife. I owe it to your memory, to myself, to our children, to make the most of my life as it is now without you.

This journey is difficult. My goal is progress—imperfect progress—because that's what's realistic. It helps to frame a lot of the changes I make as experiments or try-outs. Some work, some don't, and some evolve. This mindset helps shape this afterlife version of me. Figuring out who I am now without you. It feels like another journey—sometimes aligned with my journey through grief—and sometimes independent. I hope my desire to redefine myself will fuel the motivation I need to explore new things and grow.

Everything But Love

L: I never realized Jeff Bridges was a singer until a collection of rough cuts from the late '70s came out in 2025. I didn't spend much time with it, but it led me to his 2011 album called simply *Jeff Bridges*. These more polished tunes struck me right off. There's a song on it called "Everything but Love," a sentiment that captures the way I feel 19 months after your death.

You left me in great shape. A son and daughter. The former lives here with me and the latter is only about six miles away. Plus, our son-in-law and now a granddaughter. My sister and brother-in-law are far away, but we're closer now than ever. Our couple friends stuck with me even though I'm no longer part of a couple myself. And of course, East Cost Lucia. These are my closest connections.

My health isn't perfect, but so far, it's pretty good for my age. I have a roof over my head, food in the fridge, a lovely bulldog who sleeps with me, and time enough for myself. From the outside, one might say I have it all. I'm grateful for all I have, but some days without you I wake up and think: *Another fucking day in paradise*.

Why? Because I still miss you every day. Not all day long, but several times throughout each day. Things happen, I see things, and they remind me of you. It makes me blue. It reminds me how lonely runs deep. I feel loved, but not my lifepartner's love.

Like the song says, I've got everything, everything but love.

It's been well over a year now since you died. The shock/disbelief/denial stage has passed. I know you're really gone, and I'll never see you again. I still struggle to accept that our lives are now just my life. I try to move forward every day, but I'm not always certain I'm doing things right. I don't feel certain about what to do with the rest of my life, but I must remind myself that even now, I'm still here in the valley of grief.

Part of the healing process is grasping that I must carve out a new identity without you. It's slow going, but I think it evolves naturally over time. I will always carry you in my heart. Like a secret power, you will help me evolve into my afterlife identity. When I feel stuck in my grief, I try to remember the words "at this moment." It helps, because nothing is forever. My grief at this moment is different than it was 19 months ago. Grief evolves; it's part of this journey.

I've tried to find meaning in your death. The hard truth is, there was no meaning. It just was. Meaning can only be found in the journey after. There may be clues inside me, but finding new purpose in the afterlife may be outside myself. I must try to be open to this new world so I can better find my purpose(s) to come. I think this book is my first important step.

Whenever I find myself struggling with some aspect of grief like a regret, or a trigger, a good exercise is to imagine what it would look or feel like if I could release that regret or trigger. Am I my own worst enemy or am I the kind, forgiving person I aspire to? If I can begin with myself, it should help me with others as well.

Sometimes it's helpful to explore the opposite of my first reaction. When someone asks how I'm doing, my first thought is to explain I'm still in grief. I'm doing okay, but I'm less than I was before. The opposite would be to focus on my progress. A new book, a new idea, or a positive moment. What's the latest thing that helped me move forward?

Dragon Girls

L: We celebrated Whitney's birthday last night in Camas. Kat and Musa were there too. Great to see them. You never heard that Kat was facing her own health crisis at the ripe old age of early thirties. She is through the worst of it now, rounding the corner on a full recovery in a few months. Last night she was her exuberant self, and Musa demonstrated his typical kind-hearted demeanor. I'm grateful to count them as friends, but even more so, that they are Whitney and Sean's lifelong buds.

But I digress. After K&M departed, Whitney opened some presents. Sean gave her a wonderful LEGO set of dragons. Very cool. This got us talking about dragons and how Ann was born in the year of the dragon. We did our best to recall our own birth years' animals, and Sean checked the web to verify. I'd forgotten your birth year was also dragon. That was a bit of an epiphany, another connection between you and your granddaughter. L and Ann, both dragon girls.

You died late in 2023, and Ann was conceived in early 2024. I don't believe she is your reincarnation, but there is some sort of connection or bond between you two, perhaps only fueled by our hearts and emotions.

I think the best option for life after death is that our loved one's soul still exists, but they are not hovering over us, watching everything we do. They are engaged in their own afterlives and not directly aware of what's happening in the realm of the living. Their energy operates via the memories that still live in our hearts.

Whatever occupies my mind amplifies its importance. I think this is true for sorrow and for most things that cause me angst. When I'm able to focus my attention elsewhere for a moment or two, often the depth of my previous distress feels a little less consuming and urgent.

Stay Positive

L: Keeping a positive attitude amid the fog of grief seems daunting. In an effort to move forward I browsed a few books on the subject and found *Learned Optimism* by Martin E.P. Seligman, Ph.D. It leans clinical, but I found it worthwhile. I've always felt—or at least hoped—I was an optimist. Seligman has a test for it, which I failed miserably. But the questions are subjective, and I decided afterward that I may have failed the test, but I remain relatively optimistic. Besides, I'm in grief, and optimism is a tough extract from sorrow.

The best part of the book is its method to overcome pessimistic feelings that hold me back from taking risks or moving forward. Here's a summary:

Identify an issue and why you believe it.

For example: Without you our house is too big for me. I can't keep up with everything.

What is the result of this belief?

Despite my fond memories of living here with you; and liking a lot of things about this place, it's just too big. I will have to move.

How can you counter this belief?

Maintenance inside and out could be streamlined to make things more manageable. This could be done over time and improved as I go. Good enough would be acceptable to me. Maybe I could hire out some of the maintenance tasks.

What's the positive outlook on this issue?

I could stay here if I really want to.

Grief taxes my mental and physical health. It can trigger aches and pains, poor sleep, and over-indulging. I am trying to be mindful of these effects and counter them with exercise, eating well, and maintaining consistent sleep patterns, even when my grieving mind is not at peace.

Therapy is helpful in dealing with grief, and doctors are helpful in advising how to maintain physical health. I've also found it useful to try to change unhelpful patterns by disrupting them.

My sleep is often disrupted during the night. Rather than stress over it, I try to relax and accept reality. Sometimes that works and sometimes not. When I get too little sleep at night, I take a mid-morning or early afternoon nap. It always surprises me how an hour-long nap reinvigorates.

Loss triggers a desire to compensate. Indulgence and overindulgence can be a siren call. I've been guilty of drinking too much gin, but I was able to give it up a few months after you died. Now, I still drink, but no longer a daily cocktail.

I also still work the *NYT* daily puzzles. In a way, they are a waste of time; but I find them diverting, so I will indulge myself as long as that's the case.

Sometimes I think I distract myself with busy work on the house and yard, instead of reaching out more to old friends or making new ones. Maybe, but I also have almost twice as much to do as the before times.

I know I'm not perfect, but I have generally avoided overindulging behaviors. My daily To Do list helps me stay on track and emphasize the areas of my life I want to improve.

Grief and loss have reduced my world. It takes time for me to find the ways and means to begin to grow again. I take small steps and celebrate the act more than the result. I can't lessen my grief; I can only broaden myself. Grief has unbalanced my life. The only route to rebalance the scale is to add weight to the other side. This means making progress, moving forward. I am finding my way. I am finding success.

Dog Talker

L: Sometimes I notice how much quieter it is in the house now that I'm the only one here while Harry is away at work. The only one to talk to is Augie, and over the months I've begun talking to him more often. As much as I want to believe that your spirit still exists, I don't have visions or pick up on signs that you're still here. And if your spirit still exists, isn't it possible you have other things to do than hang around the house watching me, waiting for me to mumble under my breath that I must add bananas to the shopping list?

So I talk to the dog. What I'm really doing is talking to myself. A habit I had to break when I was a young kid, because it embarrassed me whenever I thought my sister or mother could hear me. Now it's back. Maybe it's a sign of loneliness, but I think it's more a sign of wanting to be heard. So, I talk to the dog. Not a serious one, but another side-effect of losing you.

Since I don't seem able to silence idle thoughts spoken aloud, it's not all that surprising I can't always silence my inner critic. When self-criticism blooms, it's helpful to weigh its truth. Is the point useful? Is it kind or unkind?

Sometimes I doubt my ability to move on. How well will I learn to live a fulfilling, fully engaged life without you? Thinking back to Colin's death, I know I struggled for a long time. I think by the time Whitney arrived we were able to move on pretty well. That took two to three years to occur.

After my dad died, I remember vegging out playing Yahoo games for months every night after work. I played sheepshead, cribbage, euchre, and canasta—all the card games he taught me when I was a kid. Eventually, I got tired of the few, but annoying, rude players online and quit. While it lasted, the card games honored my dad, and the escape helped me through a difficult time.

Mother's Day and Other Holidays

L: There are so many milestone dates in the wake of your death. Which should I commemorate—and how? A thanoversary is the date someone died, a remembrance day. Colin's was Nov. 26, but we always preferred to remember him in particular on his birthday, Nov. 25. Early on, I noted the 18th of every month to mark another month since your passing. Now, they sometimes slip away before I notice, because time goes by so fast.

I like lighting a candle, wearing my wedding ring, buying flowers, or drinking a couple shots of your favorite gin to commemorate you on special days like our anniversary. When Whitney and Sean are here, we have dinner together in your honor.

Today was our second Mother's Day without you. I always went out early on Mother's Day to buy you flowers and a latte. I don't remember getting flowers last year, but this year I bought a beautiful arrangement in your honor. I think of you every time I look at them on the kitchen island. They're here for you. They remind me what an exceptional mother you were for our children.

I've heard some grievers buy a gift for their missing loved one on holidays like Christmas. One widower kisses his wife's wedding ring, since he can no longer kiss her. Some people keep a place setting at the dinner table for their loved one. Others suggest starting new traditions for holidays when the old ones evoke too much sorrow.

A Native American woman recounted online that she serves a plate of food for her deceased son on his birthday. After the meal is finished, she places his paper plate on a fire in the backyard. While it burns, the smoke creates a pathway to nourish him in the hereafter.

Holidays are intended to be times of joy, so if a moment of joy appears, I embrace it. Us humans are complicated; we can experience more than one emotion simultaneously. It's possible for grief and joy to co-exist. I feel this with Ann. Joy in seeing her progress or her smile, grief because you're not here to share her love.

This is a whole 'nother area of grief. The things you're missing. All the milestones, holidays, trips, and events. I can't dwell on this void because it's useless to do so. But I can't help noting your absence either. It adds a bittersweet nuance to so many of life's pleasures. I imagine these feelings will lessen over time, but it's a fact of life today.

This year was Whitney's first celebration as a mom herself. Ann is now coming up on five months old. I didn't want to intrude on the new mom's plans, so I let her take the lead. She wanted to watch Kessler's special Mother's Day session together, so the Camas clan drove over to our house just before noon. Sean cared for Ann, while the dogs romped, and Whitney and I logged onto the event.

After a short intro, Kessler opened the floor to anyone who wanted to share. Many of the speakers were mothers who had lost their children; some very recently, some more than a year ago. Each story was sad. Everyone was trying to grapple with their loss and honor their loved one. Several brought tears to our eyes.

Holidays can be tough days for those in grief. The experts advise emphasizing the basics of self-care: eat right, hydration, limit alcohol, exercise, mindfulness, gratitude. These are the things I aim for every day without you. Around holidays, I may need to double-down but also remain realistic about what I can manage.

Those in grief often get more support or acknowledgement in the early days of loss, on those first holidays. But as the years pass, support wanes. Others have moved on, while the grieving still feel their loss, and the absence of their loved one. I reach out for support when it feels right. A lack of connections on holidays can enlarge feelings of sadness. I'm grateful for our little family.

I watched Kessler's session today to honor and reflect on your role as a mother. Afterward, we chatted and played with Ann. When she looked ready to nap, Whitney and Sean headed home, and I left to pick-up Harry at work.

Later that night, my thoughts drifted to my mom. I confess, I haven't thought so much about her in these past years. She died so long ago, over 50 years now. But death is always on my mind, and I've begun to think about the others I've lost. My mom was always so kind to me. On a few occasions as a kid, when I was deep into play with my neighborhood buddies, she would suddenly appear with a tray of snacks and drinks for me and my pals. Who does that? It made me feel like a king. She gave me a great start in life. I'm sorry she didn't live long enough to meet you and her grandchildren.

On my first Christmas without you I put up zero decorations and went without our little artificial tree. I checked in with everyone here at the time and they were all okay with that. It just didn't feel like a festive time, so I mostly ignored the holiday. We exchanged a few gifts, and as I recall Whitney made us one of your recipes, in your honor, veggie stew with dumplings.

The next year when Harry and I were alone in the house again, I brought out some decorations and put up our desktop tree on your old desk by the living room window. Harry and I both liked seeing its winking lights during those December nights. Christmas was low key again. Our granddaughter was due any day. In fact, Whitney had Ann only a few days after Christmas. Survivor's guilt returned. You would have given the world to see your granddaughter. It aches my heart to think about it, but it dominates my thoughts.

On Christmas day I watched a replay of Kessler's Heart-to-Heart zoom session. One widow who was in fifth year confirmed that things do get better as the years progress. I've always believed they would, but it's a comfort to hear a lundsman say it out loud.

Increments

L: Today marks the 20th month since you died. My sorrow and healing ebb and flow by increments. Some days it's hard to see what progress I've made. It helps to avoid words like "never" and "always" in my self-talk. I try to replace them with "now" or "at this moment." The difficult moments remain difficult, but their edges are sometimes less acute now. I attribute this to acceptance. The longer I live without you, the less able I am to be in denial. You're gone. I'm not. Like a song I heard once, so long ago, after Colin died: "I can hope, I can pray. But you've still gone away. And that's that."

Did the concept of "being seen" originate from the Black Lives Matter movement? I'm not sure, but the concept certainly occupied my consciousness during its rise. The opposite, being invisible, took a little longer. Being a woman, you dealt with invisibility all your life to one degree or another. Judith Viorst brings it up in *Making the Best of What's Left*. White men may have largely escaped feeling invisible much of their lives—except in situations of class, like when a big shot doesn't see a worker bee.

I first noted the feeling going shopping or dining with Whitney, although I didn't have the label at that time. The young, male clerk or waiter was far more interested in Whitney than me and directed their attention accordingly. I can't blame them, but it was unfamiliar territory.

Old age is universally wrapped in a cloak of invisibility. It may amplify earlier slights of race, gender, station, or health, but it will affect everyone who lives long enough. Any struggle with understanding, response, culture, or what have you, is quickly attributed to age, and patience is tried. It's self-fulfilling, as age soon becomes a signal for these deficiencies. It doesn't happen overnight. It's incremental, but once it begins it is inevitable, like aging itself.

What to do? I don't recall any countermeasures from Viorst. The best I can do is try not to practice ageism myself. When I see someone struggling, my better nature warns me to be patient and kind—and perhaps a little selfishly grateful there's someone older than me still out there.

Grief is an amplifier. It can make doing things—even routine things—more of a struggle. In struggle, old wounds can surface and feel more intense. Old wounds are negative responses to past events. My dad grew up during the great depression. As an adult he remained very frugal and cynical of any sales pitch or marketing hype. His old wound could be expressed in the thoughts, "I can do without this." or "I can't afford this." He always bought the bargain brand rather than the premium product. Sometimes that works out fine, but when a premium choice offers better quality and/or longer service, it may not.

Our conscious and subconscious minds are always trying to protect us. Sometimes old wounds drive response. In struggle or conflict, my old wounds can trigger a flight response. Rather than confronting an issue, I will rely on "the devil that I know." Examining old wounds can be helpful when I'm able to recognize them. When I explore those feelings and challenge them, it opens the door to healing and growth.

As much as I enjoy reading, I'd always been intimidated by massive tomes. I read *The Fountainhead* but couldn't even start the larger *Atlas Shrugged*. I finally got around this by reading it as an audiobook. That opened the door to many other massive volumes, which I can now read in print or audio.

I told you about my wedding ring earlier, how I finally came to the decision to take it off. I've felt less ambiguous about wearing black. I've worn a black shirt every day since you died. The only exceptions have been days like your birthday when I wore one of your T-shirts in your honor—a red one. As the two-year milestone of your death approaches, I find myself lingering over some shirts in my closet that I haven't given much thought to for months. Maybe it will be time to transition to some color after the milestone. Maybe it would be a visual reminder to myself that I'm progressing. I'll have to see how that feels...

Yard Transformation

L: One of the things we both really liked about this house was its backyard. The best view is from our bedroom window where we got a sort of aerial shot of nearly the whole spread; a large section of grass bordered by shrubs and trees. The lot is sloped a bit to the south, toward the worst section of fence. It has an oddly constructed series of steps that level off the slope near the house. They were built with heavy, treated lumber to frame the steps and filled in with pea gravel.

When Augie bulldoggie was a wee pup, he used to eat the pea gravel, so I put up a fence around the steps to keep him out. Longer-term, with your help, we boarded over the gravel, making it into a series of wooden steps. It looked better, but the steps remained a bit odd due to the varying heights of the risers and the depth of each section. The disunity of the original base annoyed even the realtor who sold us the house!

The other oddity in the landscape, that we dubbed "the stage," was an approximately 12' x 4' deck placed along the southern section of fence. Too far from the house to be useful as a deck, and too close to the street noise on that side, it seemed purposeless. I remember at some point we found an old picture of it on one of the real estate sites that showed it had originally been located on the opposite side of the yard—and somebody had actually moved it! Why? Anyway, I always wanted to get rid of it, but you were more cautious. What would we put there instead?

After you died, I continued to wrestle with the question. At first, I thought about replacing it with a gazebo. One of the detectives in a British crime show that we liked, *New Tricks*, had a gazebo in his backyard. After work, he'd often sit in it and talk to his deceased wife. I could even muse having a plaque made with your name on it.

I have talked to your spirit on certain nights, but I never notice a sign you're near. I have also written to you, for a time every night, sharing my day and signing off with love. If your spirit really is out there somewhere then I'm sure you can hear me. But the hereafter remains unproven. Am I speaking to your spirit on the other side, or the part of you that remains in my heart?

I always feared that if you ever left me, I couldn't live without you. Now, here I am trying to do just that.

As the months passed, I continued to ponder the yard from time to time, but nothing gelled, no plan began to form. I heard about a landscape designer and decided to try her. She drew up a plan that I liked, and I decided to have her make it so. To save some expense, I took on the demo. Part of the plan involved replacing the southern section of fence, which was the worst of the three sides enclosing the backyard.

It took me about two months late in 2024 to clear everything out. Part of the demo involved removing several of the improvements I'd made earlier. That felt a bit weird, but I put my faith in the designer's expertise and forged ahead. The toughest part was taking down a 60' tree and digging out all its roots. I'm hoping that'll be the last stump I ever dig out. Although I only worked two to four hours a day on the demo, I was sore every night and never fully recovered until everything was done.

Long story short, the new landscape and fence are now a reality. The designer knew the materials and plants well and transformed the yard into a sort of oasis I never could have designed myself. Everyone who's seen it marvels at the improvement and the vibe of the space. I'm glad I decided to have it done. I only wish you could've enjoyed it too. I think you would've loved it.

Summer is nearly here now. Some sunny evening—or perhaps on several sunny evenings—I will sit in one of our lawn chairs, soak in the landscape, and cherish our lives together. At least you will be here in my heart.

One of my exercises from therapy was to write you a letter telling you how I am and how I miss you. I won't repeat it here because this book is my love letter to you. The follow-on was for me to suppose that I'm you. If you were able to send me a letter from the hereafter, what would it say? A cathartic exercise, and a worthwhile release of emotion.

Almost Cut My Hair

L: I asked Whitney to cut my hair a time or two after you died. She did a great job, but it wasn't the same as when you did it. I could feel your absence, and I so missed your touch. When Whitney and Sean moved back into their house, I thought about returning to a barber. I thought about cutting it myself, but I just let it go instead. It grew longer than it had during the first year of the pandemic, before you studied videos and then started cutting it for me. After your death, my long hair felt good. It took me back to the '70s when we first met. When we were young, when we first fell in love.

Where Should I Live?

L: I admit, I've gone back and forth about our house. There are a raft of pros and cons, but the major point in favor of staying is that I like it here. The key arguments against it are 1) there's a lot to take care of, and 2) I'm certain it'll be too much for Harry when I'm gone; and it could be challenging for him to manage all the buying/selling logistics.

It's tempting to wait until something forces my hand, like navigating stairs every day or a sudden illness. Unfortunately, by that time dealing with a move may be beyond my ability. For now, I'll stay as long as I have Augie. He needs a yard. After he's gone, it may well be time for change.

Another Amendment to Forever

L: Apparently, our inability to face our own mortality has been properly documented; as I learned in Ernest Becker's *The Denial of Death*. The constant possibility of death is so overwhelming we quickly learn to repress it in childhood. Man is filled with anxiety, and fear of death is the ultimate poison. No wonder we must validate our survival by speaking in terms of forever, a concept we can't possibly grasp. What the hell does forever mean? Even in science fiction, the immortal becomes so tired of living after generations and generations of life, all he wants to do is die!

Your death shattered the protective shield of denial about mortality. But now, 22 months later, I can feel the seduction of denial inching its way into the back of my mind. Maybe I need more Pema Chödrön* to help balance the fear of death with the joy of the moment.

Count Your Dead

L: Judith Viorst has this thing where instead of counting sheep at night while trying to fall asleep, she counts her dead. *That's pretty weird* was my initial reaction, but as I gave it more thought, I came around. I've lost a lot of people during my lifetime, and I've learned to live with the losses. I fear part of that process was pushing my grief away rather than embracing it. So this idea of Viorst's was enlightening. I made a list of family you and I have lost, so that I can reflect on them from time to time and remember the good times with each person. How did I learn to live with the deaths of each one? Can I learn something from those losses that will

*See Over the Rainbow on page 107.

help me go on without you?

Your Aunt 2024, 94 years old

You 2023, 70

My Aunt 2016, 86

My Cousin 2012, 69

Your Aunt 2006, 75

My Dad 2002, 81

Your Mom 2001, 80

Your Uncle 2000, 73

My Uncle 1999, 72

Your Uncle 1996, 72

My Uncle 1995, 81

My Aunt 1994, 81

Our Son 1988, 1 day

Your Cousin 1988, 37

My Grandfather 1987, 97

Your Grandmother 1987, 99

My Grandmother 1986, 91

Your Grandmother 1983, 89

Your Dad 1978, 65

My Grandmother 1974, 81

Your Uncle 1974, 51

My Mom 1972, 51

Your Grandfather 1972, 79

My Grandfather 1970, 81

Your Grandfather 1970, 83

The serenity prayer: God grant me the wisdom to accept the things I cannot change, the strength to change the things I can, and the wisdom to know the difference.

I accept your death. There is no other choice. I never expected to have to live with it. You died with such grace. I can only hope to even approach your grace when my time comes.

I worry about our children most, although I must learn to accept my limited control. Whitney has a soulmate, and now a child of her own. I know Sean is there to care for them both, and that is a great comfort to me. I worry most for Harry. He's lost you and at some point he will lose me. I must do the best I can to pave the way for his future aloneness, but I can't arrange for every contingency. I must accept that he will have to fend for himself and figure out how to replace all the roles I play in his life. I have faith he will succeed.

The Risk of Love

L: As a child I had a few girlfriends during the school years. I went on my first date in 4th or 5th grade with a cute little girl named Bonnie. We saw a movie at the only theater in town; maybe *Son of Flubber* or some other Disney flick. It was a big deal because we held hands. Not long after she asked me to kiss her, and I flatly refused. We weren't old enough for kissing! She dumped me soon after and broke my heart.

I had several other girlfriends in the following years, none very serious, and all my relationships eventually fizzled out.

When I started college, a lot of beautiful women in my classes became friends. There were some beautiful women at the Orpheum too; where we met. I was interested in a serious relationship, not a fling. I'm sure I was a bit slow and clumsy in my approach, but I'm certain you could trust I was sincere.

Over the period of a few months we grew closer and closer. One night, in the theater's balcony, while watching a movie, I kissed you. It was just a moment before I had to go back on duty. A few days later at a party, all my pent-up passion and emotion roared out. We made out for hours, and you took me back to your place on Washington Street, where we made out for another few hours. I was all-in in love with you and thank God it was mutual. I loved you with all my heart.

As college ended, and the reality of the working world loomed, we married, and moved out west to

Oregon, where we felt our career prospects looked better. If we were wrong we could always head back to Wisconsin. But we didn't. Things worked out well in the Pacific Northwest, and we made our lives here.

Of course, I knew other women over the course of our lives. Mostly, through my various jobs. Many were attractive, and a few I really connected with, but you were always my love, and I never betrayed you.

Now that you're gone, I sometimes think about other women I've known. What would it have been like to have made a life with one of them? I miss having an intimate confidant and someone to share experiences with. I don't know if it's just another form of missing you, or if it's something more. As a fantasy, it seems okay. The reality is something else.

The best parts of my day now are escaping into our room. My first coffee in the morning, and reading after dinner, with Augie sleeping by my side.

I don't know how easy it would be to adjust to another woman, not to mention how she could put up with me! These are just random thoughts, I suppose fed by loneliness. Would true love melt away life's minor concerns? I'm not at a point where I want to explore this, but I think if somehow someone came into my life, I'd feel it.

I think I just really loved being married to you and sharing my life with you. I so miss that. The reality of someone else, rather than the fantasy, is probably not in my future.

I mentioned the Viorst book earlier. What I like best about it is that when it was written the author was 94 years old—someone who is two decades older than me! She lives in a retirement community, aka assisted living, and includes anecdotes from her neighbors and friends. The picture she paints of new relationships among seniors is riddled with cautions. Besides the normal raft of personality adjustments required, is the added threat of health issues—chronic and blossoming. A hard reality. Her cautionary tales may be more dramatic due to the age of her community (80s and up), but they are considerations. It may boil down to true love, which can overcome just about every obstacle, including logic.

She writes about one couple who fell in love. Then he was diagnosed with a serious health condition. Not wanting to burden his new girlfriend with his certain decline, he told her it would be better for them to go their separate ways. Her response was, "Too late." That's true love.

I remember the summer before my first year of college. I needed a job and answered a classified ad for a movie theater. They needed a doorman. A week went by, and I hadn't heard anything, so I called them up and asked for the manager. He said I was the first person to follow-up and hired me over the phone. You were already working there, when we met. Who could have predicted that phone call would change the rest of our lives?

I've learned that the price of love is loss; or more precisely, the risk of love is loss. When Colin died in 1988, we were nervous about another pregnancy, but not so much that it prevented us from trying again. I remember the first time we made love after he died, we both cried. What a strange mix of love, hope, and sorrow. We were thrilled a couple of years later when we learned Whitney was on her way. I was excited, but never completely relaxed until she was actually born and declared healthy.

An old neighbor miscarried her second child. She was so devastated by the loss, she and her husband never tried again. Loss colors your reality for a lifetime.

When I fell in love with you and you responded in kind, I didn't give much consideration, if any, to risk. Our love was so intoxicating, risk seemed nonexistent. Fifty years later, your death was the most devastating loss of my life.

Will I ever fall in love again? There's no way to know. I feel more ephemeral now than ever. Any new relationship would be colored by mortality. Years ago, love obliterated all concerns or hesitancies. Now, I wonder if the risks inherent in age can overcome the power of love's rewards.

For a growing number of senior women, after the death of their spouse, a life alone is their preference. They still cherish their relationships—both old and new—but they don't want to give up the freedom of being single. I may land there as well. For now, I don't feel certain of anything.

What does it take to start living again?

You once told me you admired my creative passion. I was always driven to work on some project or another. When we met it was cartooning. Later in our lives, while our children were beginning to find their own ways, I turned to writing fiction. And when I transitioned into retirement, it was self-publishing a zine about genre fiction magazines.

Without you, my passions have waned. I no longer feel the urge to continue what I began. I was always searching for an audience. I don't think I care so much about that anymore. Maybe I just wanted you to be proud of what I accomplished. Now that you're gone, it doesn't seem to matter.

So, what do I need now? Romantic love—the love of a life partner? I know I miss that, but I'm not seeking it. I know my journey to find a new life is still incomplete. I want to feel like a whole person again. Part of me died with you and I am still unable to compensate. It's natural. I'm still searching.

In therapy, I'm advised to "show up for myself." That means renewing my commitment to the changes I make. I revisit the big things from time to time, like moving to a different living situation. I take little steps to explore my options, like a stay at the beach for a week to test out what life in a coastal town might be like. How do I find meaning in this afterlife? Again, small steps, exploring options through travel, classes, volunteering, and reading. It's a process that evolves, and if something resonates, I trust I'll feel it.

Mad World

L: You watched more TV than me. Sometimes, when you discovered a great series, you encouraged me to try it, and you were always happy to join me, with what for you, would be your second viewing. These were often BBC productions like

Endeavour, *Inspector Lewis*, *Vera*, and the one I liked best, *Foyle's War*.

I noticed a series called *Three Pines* the other night. The progress bars on all eight episodes indicated they'd been seen before, but I didn't recall watching them with you. I quickly realized this was a series you'd watched alone and liked well enough to finish all eight episodes. As I began watching, it felt like unearthing a treasure. You'd left tracks and I'd followed. I know you'd enjoyed this show, and that brings even greater meaning for me. In a strange way, it felt like a shared viewing, like the ones we had so many, many nights when you were here.

In the second episode there is a sad, sad song called "Mad World," sung in French. The language you studied in school. Listening to that haunting melody suddenly sparked an interest in French. A fleeting desire, impractical, but an inkling, a longing for connection to you.

I found an English version of "Mad World" sung by Demi Lovato. Its lyrics are as melancholy as its haunting melody, It's a beautiful train wreck, and I can't help listening to its beguiling siren call. Do I listen because I'm blue? Or do I listen to feel my sorrow? This is where I seem to live so much of the time. Forgive me, my love, but I just don't know if there's any getting over losing you.

Therapy cautions me not to conflate your life with mine. Our lives were entwined, but separate. You were your own person, and I am mine. Each of us was the other's key partner in life, and however blended we felt, death made it clear we are separate. Now, I go on with only a piece of you still in my heart.

When you died, a major part of my identity quickly became "the grieving spouse." But as the months pass, I know that identity can't be what defines me. I have many identities; widower is only one. As I go on, I need to sort out what's next. I will test the waters for new things, regroup, and cautiously step out of my comfort zones. As I find what resonates, I will nurture it and move forward. The memory of you will help me through.

Carl Jung wrote: "Who looks outside, dreams; who looks inside, awakes." Either path is positive. I follow each at different times. This wisdom simply guides me where to look for each path.

Loneliness

L: One of the widower's biggest challenges is loneliness. Your absence is almost palpable, especially at certain times of the day like rising; your first cup of coffee, which I nearly always brought to you; every mealtime, the cocktail hour; TV time; and bedtime. It was hardest in the early days of grief. As time has gone by the pangs of loneliness aren't as consistent, but I still feel them as my second year without you concludes.

I never fully realized what a social/shared experience movies and television are. I'm far less interested in watching alone than when I was with you. Mark Twain wrote, "To get the full value of joy you must have somebody to divide it with." Unfortunately, this holds true for everything. Now, I retire to our room every night soon after dinner. Reading has replaced watching as my main contentment.

I'm lucky that Harry lives here. Initially, he worked nights and slept days. When he switched to working days, I liked it much better. We don't do a lot together, but just his presence in the house is comforting, and always makes me feel less lonely.

Therapists consistently rank connection as the primary prescription for loneliness. Whether it's in person, phone calls, video chats, texts, cards, or maybe even some social media; the act of reaching out and communicating helps alleviate isolation and feelings of loneliness. I think it's true. I remind myself daily, and I'm trying to increase my efforts to reach out. I have a ways to go, but I guess recognizing the need is the first step in filling it.

It can be uncomfortable to reach out. It can feel awkward, but it's part of the re-creation of life here in the afterlife.

Even the writings of widows and single women who aren't looking for a partner, all say their connections keep them from feeling lonely. And on the rare occasions when they do, they just double-down and try something new like a class, volunteer work, or seeing if they might turn an acquaintance into a friend. As my grieving friend Les points out, even connecting for a moment at the coffee shop or grocery store can feel refreshing—a moment of normalcy in a world which is no longer normal.

Another bit of advice the experts extol is get a pet. I'm lucky that we got our bulldog about 18 months before you died. His companionship provides far more than the effort required for his keep. Most nights he sleeps with me, and that is his greatest blessing to help me through these all-too-frequently lonely nights. Harry is at his most helpful in caring for Augie. I'm grateful he has taken on the lion's share of bathing, nail-trimming, and late-night trips outside.

Margareta Magnusson, in *The Swedish Art of Aging Exuberantly* reiterates the value of pets. However, she was 86 and living in a studio apartment when she wrote it. She admits at her age, the responsibility of a cat or dog is too much for her. Instead, she dotes on houseplants, including one-way conversations. She reports they help her feel less lonely.

My other companion is books. I love them. I feel better when I'm surrounded by bookshelves filled with books. Since you died, I've read or listened to an almost unbroken stream of nonfiction titles about grief, loss, connection, living alone, optimism, creativity, and downsizing. I alternate with crime fiction, so I get plenty of adventurous escape as well. For me, the solitary act of reading fits my new single life better than anything else I've found. In fact, reading is the only thing I've found that doesn't seem changed by your death.

Earlier in my grief journey, your suffering as death approached, and my sorrow afterward, dominated my thoughts. Once my mind was fixated on these things, it was difficult to find relief. Distraction was the greatest help. Grief can feel slightly less intense when you're able to release its hold for a few moments.

After nearly two years, my memories of your death no longer dominate my thoughts of you. Now memories of our good times arrive more often, and things I hadn't thought of in years, emerge. These are positive signs of progress and acceptance.

I always welcome you in my dreams, but early on they were all nightmares as my fitful sleep always returned to your final weeks. As time goes on, this occurs less often. One night I dreamt of you before waking. I held you in my arms and kissed your neck and cried. I'm still in love with you.

Second Thanoversary

L: I have anticipated this day with dread, uncertain of how it would feel once it actually arrived. I think more than anything I just wanted it to come and go as quickly as possible. I slept fitfully the night before, wondering if I should have set the alarm for 1:15 AM when you died two years ago. Augie was restless too and that no doubt contributed to all the night's interrupted sleep. But animals can be very perceptive to currents we don't discern. Perhaps there was something external in the air driving my anxiety.

At times when I woke, I gazed across the bed at the silhouette of the fame with your picture and the lilies I bought yesterday, atop the desk. I got up once to look out through the picture window down at the yard, dimly lit in reflected lights from nearby porches and the streetlamp in front of our neighbor's house.

If I was hoping to catch a glimpse of your spirit or sense your presence in our room, I discerned nothing but the knowledge you were gone, and had been for two years.

I woke at 3:00 AM, made tea and read the headlines. As the day progressed, rudderless, I busied myself with routine. Nothing important, but at least I didn't sit and mope the entire day. You remained on my mind every hour.

I stopped at times to ponder the day but must confess I'm at a loss to identify exactly what I'm feeling or what I'm supposed to feel on this second thanoversary. It is only the aching human heart that places such weight on this ethereal milestone of that accursive day.

At night I usually read, but on this night I listened to my mourning playlist, thought of your lovely heart, and bid you farewell yet again.

Latency

Grief waits in latency to surface. Three weeks

after your second thanoversary it hit me again as hard as the morning you died. I'll blame it on Patty Loveless' "I Don't Want to Feel Like That." Most of its lyrics resonant, but there were two lines that broke me:

I can't think one thought that doesn't start with your name.

I can't see one day that isn't more of the same.

Just like the song's opening verse, I cried myself to sleep that night, waking up well before the first light. I have no explanation for this but latency. Your death demolished me again. I suppose sobbing was a helpful release, but it also took me by surprise. I thought I'd made such progress, but I guess that's grief. The stealthy archer ready to skewer your heart whenever something triggers his arrow.

Since that cathartic release, things have been better. I feel like the valley is no longer where I dwell full time. I may never escape its pull, but I feel like I'm back on level ground more of the time. Forward, I go.

My Afterlife

I have lived without L for over two years. The intense sorrow of early grief has eased. It's dissipated, but still present. The waves are calmer now and less frequent. This is progress in the journey. Experts offer: "Don't dwell on the pain, focus on the memories." I try to keep this in mind.

We all practice varying degrees of self-acceptance, but I think the goal in grief is to fully accept ourselves and our feelings about our loss.

Like life itself, grief evolves. Working through grief means fully grieving. In life we strive to fully live, but how often do we arrive? I think the same applies to grief. Fully feeling our grief is difficult. In the moments I feel it most intensely, I also find hesitation. Who welcomes pain and sorrow? I think this hesitancy is natural and protective. I think this is why after two years, I still grieve. Loss takes time to settle into your bones.

I can be anywhere when the whisper of a memory surfaces and I'm reminded once again that I'm alone. A deep sigh wells up as sorrow sweeps across my mind. I try to shrug it off and be present. Sometimes I can. Sorrow is deep feelings of sadness, and they have nowhere to go.

I think the sharpest edges of grief are worn through time spent with loss and trying to understand its mysteries. Kessler affirms the final stage of grief is to find meaning. He wrote a book and a workbook about it. I can see this in my friend Craig, whom I wrote about in the introduction. When Craig's wife died he found he could no longer work in his chosen career. The work felt empty. He wanted meaningful employment and found it supporting patients in a care center.

For me, accepting loss means reconciling it. Not denial—I will always grieve my losses—but I know I can never change them. I'm learning to spend more energy on moving forward and less on trying to hold onto what I cannot change.

In early grief, the idea of time as a healer can be offensive. Time is deceiving. It seems to drag when grief is new, and yet it always moves along in the background. Suddenly, one day you realize it's been two months, then three, etc. Maybe that's why people say time is elastic. It can seem to drag and race simultaneously.

I think time inherently prods us to live in the present. Grief prods us to live in the past. With time's encouragement we can heal. Our grief leaves scars we never forget, but with time we can learn to be more present and accept the past as passed. Moving forward is difficult. When we picture progress, it's smooth. In reality, progress is bumpy.

I read *Oldster Magazine* on Substack. The seniors interviewed always extol that the wisdom they've gained over a lifetime of experience makes them less prone to error. I think grief shatters that belief. I've made so many mistakes over the last two years. Maybe that's because my "better half" wasn't here to ground or balance me. The jolt from *we* to *me* capsized my equilibrium. I still believe wisdom can grow from failure, but life widowed—life in grief— is a setback that shakes every foundation.

Living with ambiguity is the challenge. I want closure. But closure is alien to grief. Ambiguity is not. We wish for the dead to rest in peace, but survivors must learn to as well. We must learn how to hold on and let go in the same breath, at the same time.

Ambiguity is why figuring out what to do with all the stuff, the old photos, mementos, and possessions is vexing. I just want it done with. I have faith I'll get there eventually, but it takes time and patience and effort. When I focus on what's been dealt with, instead of what remains, it helps.

There is no closure to loss. We can learn to accept it, but its scars remain. We have no choice but to live with the fact that life will never be as it was.

Writing this book has been my purpose over the last six or seven months. Now that it's coming to an end, I realize again that my afterlife is confronting me. Two years in grief have passed. I can no longer just cocoon and retreat under the blanket of sorrow. I need to have a life in my remaining days. I cannot stay here for the rest of what remains. I need to define my new self and discover what will nurture my spirit.

That's the big question: What now?

A useful tool in recovery is to explore your feelings via the question: What would [   ] be like if [   ]? For me it's "What would [my afterlife] be like if [I were fully living]?

I've been best when my moments were filled with taking action. What's hardest is knowing what to do when the moments are unfilled. With L, there were fewer of these moments since her presence and needs held my attention. Without her my idle moments are more frequent and stretch into hours. How do I fill them? How do I decide what things to do, and how do I motivate myself to do them?

Who am I without L?

My process is to revisit my Ten Tools for Embracing Your Finitude from Burkeman's book*. Part of this involves venturing out to try new things and pushing my comfort zones. The path is unpaved, my direction may change, the inevitable setbacks could be difficult, but to move forward, to progress is the success. The destination *is* the journey.

I've been wearing a black shirt for two years in remembrance of my love, my sweet L. It's time to stop and add some color to my wardrobe. The routines and rituals that honor L are imperative, but it's healing for me to start some routines and rituals that affirm my new life alone as well.

I will continue to write to L, sharing thoughts, emotions, and successes. I will enrich my connection to family and friends and stay open to potential new friends. I'll work to maintain my health and home and reduce my possessions for an eventual move to smaller quarters—a townhouse or condo. I'll pursue outlets that nurture my creative spirit, and I will reach out for peace and love. For only love is real.

Uff da, indeed.

-Kenneth Richardson

*See Recovery Bookshelf

Grief Bookshelf

A Grief Observed by C.S. Lewis, Harper One, 2015 The famous author's thoughts on the death of his wife.

Finding Meaning: The Sixth Stage of Grief by David Kessler, Scribner, 2019 Where to look to find meaning after the death of a loved one.

Finding Meaning: The Sixth Stage of Grief Workbook by David Kessler, Bridge City Books, 2024 Prompts and guidance to chart your search for meaning in the afterlife of loss.

Naming the Ghost by Emily Hockaday, Cornerstone Press, 2022 Poems inspired by the author's loss of her father and the birth of her daughter.

Poetry as Survival by Gregory Orr, University of Georgia Press, 2002 How poetry aids those in mourning, plus a guide to understanding the giants of verse.

When Things Fall Apart by Pema Chödrön, Shambhala, 1997 A Buddhist nun offers advice and love for life's toughest challenges, like loss.

Why Me? Coping with Grief, Loss, and Change by Pesach Krauss and Morrie Goldfischer, Bantam Books, 1988 Lessons for living with a devastating loss.

Year of Magical Thinking, The by Joan Didion, Alfred A. Knopf, 2005 The famous author's thoughts on the death of her husband and the life-threatening illness of her daughter.

Dancing at the Pity Party by Tyler Feder, Dial Books, 2020 A cartoonist's graphic novel about the death of her mother and her grief journey.

Recovery Bookshelf

10% Happier by Dan Harris, Dey St., 2014 The famous newsman's search for enlightenment and his discovery of meditation.

Big Magic by Elizabeth Gilbert, Riverhead Books, 2015 Inspiration for creative pursuits.

Embracing the Unknown: Life Lessons from the Tibetan Book of the Dead by Pema Chödrön, Sounds True (Audiobook), 2019 Accepting the impermanence of our world.

Four Agreements, The: A Practical Guide to Personal Freedom by Don Miguel Rulz, Amber-Allen Publishing, 1997 A guide to holding steady in a world of chaos.

Four Thousand Weeks: Time Management for Mortals by Oliver Burkeman, Picador, 2021 Figuring out what's important and how to spend more of your limited time on it.

Learned Optimism: How to Change Your Mind and Your Life by Martin E.P. Seligman, PH.D., Vintage Books, 2006 A research-based exploration for nurturing an optimistic outlook.

Learning to Live Alone by Bob Nurmence, iUniverse, 2007 A widower's journey in making his way in the world without his wife.

Living Alone and Loving It by Barbara Feldon, Touchstone, 2003 Part memoir, part guidebook for a single life.

Making the Best of What's Left by Judith Viorst, Simon & Shuster, 2025 Thinking past age and loneliness.

Platonic: How the Science of Attachment Can Help You Make — and Keep — Friends by Marisa G. Franco, Ph.D., G.P. Putnam's Sons, 2022 A research-based approach to connection.

Stoic Mindset, The: Living the Ten Principles of Stoicism by Mark Tuitert, St. Martin's Essentials, 2024 An Olympic champion introduces the stoic virtues of wisdom, courage, justice, and temperance.

Swedish Art of Aging Exuberantly, The: Life Wisdom from Someone Who Will (Probably) Die Before You by Margareta Magnusson, Scribner, 2022 Part memoir, part guidebook for making the most of your remaining senior life.

Three Secrets of Living Alone, The by Phyllis Ledewitz Press, Self-Published 2013 Getting from loss to living comfortably alone is a journey of indeterminate length. This short guide provides a possible framework for your path.

Who Will Cry When You Die? by Robin Sharma, Jaico Publishing, 2006 Inspiration to help guide a happier life.

Practical Optimism by Sue Varma, M.D., Avery, 2024 A guidebook for a more optimistic perspective on life.

Afterlife Bookshelf

Born Again: The Truth About Reincarnation by Hans Holzer, Pocket Book 1973 Research-based evidence for reincarnation.

Nothing to Fear: Demystifying Death to Live More Fully by Julie McFadden, RN, Tarcher, 2024 A hospice nurse explains the mechanics of death.

Proof of Heaven: A Neurosurgeon's Journey into the Afterlife by Eben Alexander, Simon & Shuster, 2012 The ultimate near-death experience.

Spook: Science Tackles the Afterlife by Mary Roach, W.W. Norton, 2005 The author's journey to uncover the truth about an afterlife.

When Bad Things Happen to Good People by Harold S. Kushner, Avon 1983 Rabbi Kushner redefines his God to fit the realities of senseless death, suffering, and heartbreaking loss.

Mourning Playlist

Of the novels, movies, and music we consume, I think we internalize their characters, stories, and words. We hear their meaning through our own experiences and our current reality. When we're falling in love, the scenes and verses of our media are seen through that lens. When we're in mourning, it's the same.

These are the songs gathered over the months of my first two years in grief. Many of these were written about the loss of a relationship, but it's easy to reframe them as a loss due to death. In some cases, nearly all the lyrics are applicable, while in others it's simply the chorus or a single, resonant line. For me, they all express part of the sorrow and sadness I feel without L.

"Fields of Gold" Eva Cassidy *Songbird*

"Useless Desires" Patty Griffin *Impossible Dream*

"What'll I Do" Linda Ronstadt *What's New*

"Let Go" Allison Moorer *Miss Fortune*

"Two of Us" The Beatles *Let It Be*

"I Don't Want to Feel Like That" Patty Loveless *Long Stretch of Lonesome*

"Your Long Journey" Robert Plant & Alison Krauss *Raising Sand*

"Harvest Moon" Neil Young *Harvest Moon*

"I Don't Know How to Say Goodbye (Bang Bang Boom Boom)" Dwight Yoakam & Post Malone *Brighter Days*

"Baby I'm Blue" Hal Ketchum *I'm the Troubadour*

"Long Ride Home" Patty Griffin *1000 Kisses*

"Can You Hear Me Call" Ringo Starr & Molly Tuttle *Look Up*

"Everything But Love" Jeff Bridges *Jeff Bridges*

"Mad World" Demi Lavato *Dancing with the Devil*

"Tell Heaven" Rosanne Cash *The River & The Thread*

"Only Love is Real" Carole King *Thoroughbred*

"Over the Rainbow" Judy Garland *The Wizard of Oz Soundtrack*

NOKdoc Topic List

Intro
My Body
Executor / Taxes
Notification
  Family
  Friends
  Groups / Associations
  Others
Lawyer
Legal Documents
Health Insurance
House
Passwords
Virus Protection
File Cabinets
Bank / Investment Records
Financial Accounts / Assets
Service Record
Pension
Social Security
Fraternal Organizations
Cell Phone
Internet
Garbage
Natural Gas
Electricity
Water
Property Tax
Income Tax
Newspapers
Credit Cards
Irrigation System
Auto License Tags
Furnace / Heat Pump
Instructions / Directions (appliances, etc.)
Vendors / Services
Gas Fireplaces
Yard Care

Garage Door Opener
Plumbing
Electrical
Tools
Thermostat
Pet(s)
Software Subscriptions
Maintenance Care Agreements
Cloud Storage
eBay, Etsy, etc.
PayPal/Venmo
Email Accounts
Website/Blog
Social Media
Video Streaming Services
Other Subscriptions
Phone Apps
Collection(s)
Personal Items
Birthdays
A Few Thoughts on Losing a Loved One
Household Maintenance
Grief Library

Acknowledgments

Leslie Berry
Tim Joy
John Kuharik
Bob Snashall